When You're Ready Boys - Take Hold!

My Grappling Story

Len Ironside

authorHOUSE®

AuthorHouse™ UK Ltd.
500 Avebury Boulevard
Central Milton Keynes, MK9 2BE
www.authorhouse.co.uk
Phone: 08001974150

©2011 Len Ironside. All rights reserved.

No part of this book may be reproduced, stored in a retrieval system, or transmitted by any means without the written permission of the author.

First published by AuthorHouse   05/05/2011.

ISBN: 978-1-4520-8950-8 (sc)

Any people depicted in stock imagery provided by Thinkstock are models, and such images are being used for illustrative purposes only. Certain stock imagery © Thinkstock.

This book is printed on acid-free paper.

Because of the dynamic nature of the Internet, any Web addresses or links contained in this book may have changed since publication and may no longer be valid. The views expressed in this work are solely those of the author and do not necessarily reflect the views of the publisher, and the publisher hereby disclaims any responsibility for them.

Wrestling has been in my blood ever since I can remember. Even at school I used to take away the legs of an opponent to combat my lack of height. Or run away with some bully following close behind me, when suddenly I would drop down into a ball. They would usually tumble over the top of me and I was on them like a flash! Applying some kind of arm-twist or leg manoeuvre which would have them yelling for me to stop.

It was around 1961 when Independent television came to Aberdeen. Grampian was and still is the local Station. Although television was a fairly new phenomenon in our house, the coming of Independent television, with its artificial adverts was treated as final proof that Aberdeen had entered the 20th century.I used to sit glued to the screen on a Saturday afternoon at 4.0pm watching, living and learning every move.

The first bout I ever saw was between "Dazzler" Joe Cornelius, a handsome, curly haired grappler who wore black tights and a cheeky smile; and his opponent Roy "Bull" Davis, a shaven headed hard man who scowled and grunted throughout the contest. Little did I know that same hard man Davies was to be the referee in a crucial wrestling contest some 20 years later. Strangely enough it was the villain of the piece, Roy "bull" Davis, whom I remember so vividly shouting," No Joe, No! NO! Joe. Not my arm!" That memory haunted me ever since and hooked me into the world of wrestling.

I was fortunate enough to have an Uncle, called Stewart Ross, who was a sign writer to trade. He was employed by the local authority. One of his duties was to arrange the large white letters inside the glass advertising cabinet, which announced the top of the bill contest to be shown later that week in the Music Hall on Union Street. Because of this, and as he was well known to the Music Hall staff, Uncle Stewart got free entry to the wrestling which took place every Tuesday during the summer months in Aberdeen. I was later to discover that this had more to do with the promoter George De Relwyskow, himself a former World amateur lightweight Champion, having a girlfriend in Aberdeen, rather than the economics of putting on wrestling contests! Nonetheless, the Music Hall had packed houses of around 1300 people and almost 300 of them were standing. Being only a wee chap (I was nearly 11 years old!) I had the privilege of sitting on my Uncles shoulders. The bad news was that this only operated during the first half of the bill.During the interval, Uncle Stewart visited the nearest pub and was never in a fit state to allow me on top of his shoulders subsequently. When I grew older he managed to get us seats near the front row this was more comfortable and decidedly more reliable. I never remembered the first live wrestling I saw but there were certainly some very fine grapplers around.

One of my heroes was Dennis Mitchell from Bradford who with his short blonde hair and spotless white trunks, he always reminded me of an overgrown baby.In those early years I loved to watch the Scottish Heavyweight Champion Ian Campbell punish the English heroes. In those days the heavyweight talent was much the same calibre. There was little to chose between the top twenty wrestlers. Because of this, the Heavyweight title of Great Britain changed hands rather a lot. Big Ian had been British Champion on several occasions, never really holding the title for very long. Other heavies like Billy Joyce, Albert 'Rocky' Wall, and Welshman Gwyn Davies all had their spell as British Champion. Ian Campbell, along with Scottish lightweight Champion Jimmy McKenzie, obtained a bit part in the cult movie "the Wicker Man" starring Christopher Lee, Brit Eckland and Edward Woodward.

Big Ian had been a great ambassador for wrestling and Scotland in general. He had even tried, and nearly succeeded, in bringing the American World Wrestling Champion, Bruno Samartino to these shores to defend his title. Samartino was a real living legend, who regrettably never came to the U.K. Campbell always did so well amongst his own people, taking on the best in the division and giving them a very rough ride.Sadly I heard of his death through heart failure in his home in Argyll. His massive 20 stone bulk had been reduced to a mere 9 stone. A sad end to a man who had been a giant in the ring with a heart of gold outside it. He performed many fine work for charities and had been a very amusing after dinner speaker.But the man I admired most then and still to this day was the incomparable George Kidd. He was only 10 stone 8 Lbs (67 kilos) but this Houdini of the ring was a master of his craft. Probably the reason why he held the World Wrestling Title for an unprecedented 26 years. A feat unheard of, and unequalled, in any other sport. He was to play a role in my wrestling career much later on. Never in my wildest dreams did I ever imagine our paths would cross at a date in the future. More about George later.

The Scottish wrestlers were few in number, but they more than made up for this in quality. The strongest Scottish team was lead by Ian Campbell who was accompanied by Chic Purvey, the hard bitten middleweight champion of Scotland, Clayton Thompson, a smooth perfectionist who held 5 titles at different weights at the same time; and Ted Hannon who was a workmanlike performer in the ring. All this was capped by the World Champion from Dundee, George Kidd. This team was never beaten in over 20 contests. But we have never been able to field such a strong team since. These then were the idols that influenced me. I would have followed them to the ends of the earth just to see them in action. I watched and I learned.I often used to grapple with my close friend Jim Knox and his brothers. We were all wrestling daft and spent hours practising moves and perfecting holds. We would then challenge the local kids from our area to a" no holds barred" contest. It was so much more exciting than football! In these far off days we all wanted to be grapplers who would one day appear on World of Sport hosted by Dickie Davis! There were no wrestling clubs in Aberdeen and so I had to travel for on the mat training.

I wrote to the secretary of the amateur wrestling association asking for the names of club secretaries throughout Scotland. The nearest coach was in Perth, some 80 miles from Aberdeen. I didn't drive at that time so I decided to hitch hike to Perth every Sunday for 3 hours of coaching. The chap who put me through my paces was a Ross Caruthers. He was originally from Kent but had settled in Perth because of his job. Ross was 6 feet 2 inches tall and weighed in at around 14 1/2 stone (Kilos) Given that I was only 5 foot 3 inches high and weighed a mere 10 stone 12 pounds (68 kilos) at that time you can imagine that I had some very hard lessons to learn. Nonetheless I was determined to tough it out.

I entered an open competition which was held in the Caird Park in Dundee. I was so desperate to put my training to the test. It was held in the open air and fortunately the weather was brilliant. I came out on top to win the "Crown of Scotland" trophy, it was the first of many. But, more importantly, I met some gritty wrestlers from Dundee who were keen as mustard and steeped in the traditions of wrestling. I struck up a friendship and made frequent visits to their club. It was owned by the railwaymen and they allowed the wrestlers the use of a back room every Monday and Tuesday evening. I trained with them and Caruthers for nearly 2 years and I remember how much I enjoyed the summer weekends travelling round the highland games circuits challenging all comers to catch as catch can contests. I met some very interesting people on those circuits and used the experience to develop my own style and moves. It was during one of those sunny Sunday afternoons I was "discovered" by the Lightweight maestro George Kidd. He told me he liked what he saw and I was invited to some of his training sessions, some thing which was most unusual for Kidd. George was very fussy about where he trained and who saw him. He took me down to London to meet a real gentleman called Joe D'Orazio. Joe was a proper gent who had forgotten more about wrestling than most grapplers learn in a lifetime. Joe was a great all rounder. He was a poet, an actor, a writer and a referee. His knowledge was vast and he had an intellect to match. Like many men at that time, when Joe left the forces he took up wrestling. His life long friend being the fellow Bermondsey grappler, Iron Man Steve Logan. Joe had so many interlinked careers. I never heard a bad word said against him, and if you had ever met him you would see why. He was friendly, helpful, and honest and always concerned about other people's problems, hence the amount of money he used to raise for charity. The world was a better place thanks to people like Joe D'Orazio. Joe coached me in some falls, locks and general ring craft. Then around 1973 with Kidd's help I made contact with Max Crabtree.

    Max was a tall, smooth, quietly spoken Yorkshireman, who had been a professional wrestler himself but was now trying his hand at promoting the sport. He had been an underling to George De Relwyskow and very often did not get the top of the bill grapplers for his bills because Relwyskow & Green promotions took first pick. Max had two brothers; Shirley, yes Shirley, taken from the book "Cat on a hot tin Roof," a 25 stone giant of a man, and Brian who was a respected referee with more than a little skill in grappling and acrobatics. Max, as the underling of George De Relwyskow, went to seek out his own brand of talented wrestlers. Promoters are a very jealous lot. They want the big names in the sport to top their bills and couldn't really care about any struggling new promoters. Crabtree phoned me and discussed the prospect of me having a professional bout. He wanted me to be clear that if I accepted, I could never return to the ranks of the amateur. He also told me he couldn't pay me for the bout, (how typical of British Promoters!) claiming he wanted to see how well I would do first before signing any contracts. I only too willingly agreed to this on the condition that I was given petrol money. I sent Max my picture and my personal details. It was nearly 3 weeks later that I received a letter saying I was to appear in the Eldorado Stadium in Edinburgh against one of the Eldorado All Stars, Dave Ramsden from Yorkshire. I was over the moon. It seemed that all my boyhood dreams had come true. I would get my big break at last!

Following 6 years in the amateur ranks and a series of Highland games circuits, I was finally getting my professional break at the Eldorado Stadium in Edinburgh. George Kidd had given me some advice and had polished up the rough edges and seemed greatly encouraged by my unique style. It was a style which used my opponents weight against himself, and it was based on the European style of wrestling known as Greco Roman.

Eldorado was one of the doyens of wrestling and boxing. It was hailed, not only in Scotland but throughout the length and breadth of the United Kingdom. You can imagine my surprise when I discovered that the venue was so old that it resembled a cowshed! You could actually see the sky through the holes in the roof. Nonetheless, Scotland's premiere venue and my first paid contest for which I was not paid! Max Crabtree the promoter, who was the older brother of Shirley Crabtree better known as big Daddy, had matched me against Dave Ramsden. He had been around the rings for about 15 years and was part of a popular team known as the Eldorado All Stars. Ramsden weighed 11 stone (69.8kilos) 70 kilos) and was 5 foot 5 inches tall. First into the ring came Ramsden much to the cheers of the Edinburgh crowd. Although from Yorkshire they treated him like one of their own. Then the a local Piper played "Scotland the

Brave" and I entered the ring down the long walk from the dressing rooms. There were gasps all round. People could hardly believe that a guy who barely measured 5 foot 3 inches could possibly be prepared to tackle wrestlers in the ring. It was a great disappointment to me that as I entered the ring I heard some guffaws of laughter. Don't get me wrong. I enjoy a good laugh and I like comedians, just like the next person, but there is no place for them in the ring. I had names shouted at me like "Tom Thumb" The "Wee Nipper," and the "Ferret." None of which endeared themselves to me! I felt like an outcast! However, Once the bell sounded I tore across the ring like a tiger. Throughout my career I have always believed in putting brains before brawn. I try to out think opponents and use moves which they seldom see and therefore have difficulty in countering. But on this first occasion my only thought was to win, and to do it in the shortest possible time. I have to say my enthusiasm boiled over and I frequently picked Ramsden off the canvas when he was down, just to get on with the bout. My tactics did nothing to endear me to the crowd. Strangely enough, in later years the Edinburgh crowd became very partisan behind me when I faced wrestlers in their venue. But on that cold evening they would have felt I was a very nasty piece of work! The contest ended when I grabbed the referee, Brian Crabtree, yet another brother of Big Daddy, and tied him in the ropes, to prevent him interfering with the bout and thus allowing me to finish off the job of work I had begun on Dave Ramsden.

Needless to say I was disqualified and left the ring in disgrace. Despite that, the promoter was impressed by my gutsy performance and saw a potential in me which was later to win me 3 titles.

One grappler who was shouting my praises saying "This Guys Magic" and "He'll tear their Fuc..ing ears off" was the powerful and extremely charismatic Andy Robbin. He loved a fight more than a wrestling match and is one of those larger than life characters. Robin was known as "The Mad Axe man" by his fellow professionals on account of him being a woodcutter to trade and having a wild sense of humour. Andy was so strong he trained with weights which would have been recognised as world records and he didn't even break into a sweat. I remember one heavyweight saying," he doesn't just take hold of you to throw, he puts his powerful hands right through you!"

Andy Robbin had been one of my boyhood heroes. He took great delight in jumping the ring and challenging the top heavyweight wrestlers of the day. This was all the more bold because Andy was only 5 foot 9 in height and weighed a mere 14 stone(90 Kilos) in those days. Andy won the Commonwealth Mid Heavyweight title in Canada, in 1966 when in front of a crowd of 12,000 people when he defeated Doug Noble of Edmonton. He had worked his way through 20-contest eliminator to gain that privilege. It was while in Canada Andy acquired his speciality hold the "Powerlock." He was taught it by an old Sioux Indian Chief who despite his age Andy claims was a supple as a monkey! That Powerlock move is one that could win any bout. So much so, that Andy offered £1000 to anyone who could break the hold and after some 28 years- there have been no takers. But sheer power and guts got him through and the crowd love his style, which was very fast for a heavy man. He seldom ever lost and one of the best contests I ever saw him in was against the Japanese giant Shozo Kobayashi. Big Shozo was 6 feet 4 inches tall and weighed some 21 stone. (133 Kilos) Not an ounce of fat on his body. He had been brought to this country by George De Relwyskow and his fierce reputation was crushing all before him. His famous finishing move was a double handed chop to the head. More often than not I have seen big men fall to their knees clutching their heads, which were pouring with blood. Such was the power of the man.

Andy Robbin cared nothing of this. He attacked the Jap with a vengeance, doing all he could to irritate him, slapping his face, patting his head and even rubbing the whitener off his boots on to the giants face. Both wrestlers had gained a fall each and the bout ended in a draw. But the Jap knew he had been in a battle and Andy enhanced his growing reputation. They were to meet once again before Shozo left these shores, and although the contest wasn't technically so good, Andy beat the Giant in an action packed thriller.

Andy loved the aggression in me and said to the promoter Max Crabtree, patting firmly on the head as only Andy could do," Give him a title chance now. There's no one around to stop him." It seems strange looking back now that on that first evening, I got the cold shoulder from 2 other Scots wrestlers, Jim McKenzie who was the Scottish Lightweight Champion, and Bill Ross who was later to become a close Friend and indeed a very successful tag partner of mine. We also did some classes for the boy scouts in the local scout hall in Drumoak, a village outside Aberdeen. And some years later we ran a personal self defence class for the Grampian Police new recruits. But that initial meeting was cold. There is nothing worse than professional jealousy and both McKenzie and Ross recognised a future threat. I learned a lot of lessons that evening. I changed my approach immediately. I listened intently to what George Kidd had to tell me and from that day onward I thoroughly enjoyed my wrestling career. In over 300 bouts I was only ever disqualified twice. But these are very different stories.

Weeks later, following that extraordinary bout I was given the chance to return to the Eldorado stadium, only this time I adapted my attitude and kept my head. I grappled with a man called Iron Lew Roberts, from Crewe. He was a solid workmanlike wrestler, weighing in at around 12 stone (76 kilos) I defeated him by 2 straight falls in rounds 4 and 5.This time the cheers were ringing in my ears. Believe me that is the sweetest sound in the world.

Up until now I had been fortunate enough to have Borrowed my father's car. It was a red Toledo. A rather heavy vehicle, which was quite hard on the petrol. My father, who enjoyed all sports but never had much time for wrestling, made it clear that he could not afford the huge numbers of miles, which would be inevitably forced on his car in my journeys to and from the halls of Scotland. I could not have agreed with him more, so he and I set about looking for a reasonably cheap vehicle, which wouldn't cost the earth to run. I eventually settled on a small white mini, which cost me all of £600. This was in 1973 when my petrol bill for Edinburgh came to £5.00. and that was both ways!

One of the most harrowing weeks I have ever experienced came, not through wrestling, but at the hands of that little innocent mini. Strangely enough, both in the same week. Because most of the large promoters lived in the south and midlands, Scotland was quite a distance to travel weekly by car. They therefore decided to set up circuits in alternative weeks. The main run was Edinburgh, Perth, Aviemore, Stirling, followed by Dunfermline, Dundee, Elgin .The Third week was usually Aberdeen on Tuesday and Kelvin Hall,

Glasgow on Thursday. As well as these venues there were the occasional bills in places like Kelso, Orkney, Ayr and Falkirk. Although all these were organised under the banner of Joint Promotions, George De Relwyskow ran Aberdeen himself and left his side kick, Max Crabtree to do the rest. That gave Crabtree the extensive travelling around, and old George only travelled to Aberdeen. Promoters had to be clever enough and innovative enough to keep half of the bill on the circuit whilst changing the opponents. And all of this had to be at a very low cost level. Joint Promotions never wanted to pay out too much petrol money. It was therefore of great benefit to have a large pool of Scottish grapplers who could travel and compete all round Scotland. This was particularly useful when they ran one off spectaculars in Wick, Kirkcaldy Ice Rink, Paisley Ice Rink, Falkirk and Inverness. (They usually had annual tournaments in those locations because there weren't enough people to come to a regular monthly promotion)

It was the winter of '73 and I had to wrestle twice in the week before Christmas. I was trained up to peak and looking forward to presenting myself in a good light. I had never wrestled before in Dunfermline nor Elgin, which was only 65 miles from home. I wanted to do exceptionally well. However on the Wednesday I took quite a heavy cold and was feeling a bit woozy. Nonetheless, I left work early and drove to Dunfermline. The journey was around 124 miles. It was not snowing but very frosty.

I arrived at the Kinema Ballroom where wrestling was held those days and began to do my warm up routine. This was simply a limited Circuit consisting of 30 press-ups, 100 squats, 30 sit- Ups, 100 step-ups 30 back raises and 50 burpees. this was done three times. However, unusually I felt a bit lethargic and rather sick inside, probably due to the cold. Nevertheless, I took a couple of dodo tablets to help my breathing and a swig of cough mixture. This was probably the worst thing I could have done.

I wrestled a bloke called Sid Cooper that evening. He was a villain of the highest order who held no respect for novices. Sid weighed 12 1/2 stone (79.3 kilos) and loved to bend the rules. The bout itself wasn't a bad one. Cooper had little skill and I was able to run him ragged in the first 3 rounds. I outsmarted him in round 4 and took a pin fall off him to open the scoring. This was all too much of a humiliation for Sid and he went berserk in the 5th round forcing referee Crabtree (Brian that is) to disqualify him. As I returned for a shower I felt sick and my insides were giving me hell. This was more due to the effects of the medicine coursing through my blood rather than anything I had suffered at the hands of Sid Cooper. In fact in today's game I might even have tested positive in a drugs test! That was the easy part of my evening. I had been on first so I was able to hurry off early in order to get home.

The snow was beginning to fall more thickly now and I was anxious to get going. I drove for several miles before I noticed the red ignition light showing. Being more than a little ignorant about the mechanics of a car. As far as I was concerned, as long as you filled it with petrol every so often, it usually worked! I assumed that the little red light was shinning because the engine had been cold. More and more miles passed and still the light shone brightly. I put the heater on full but the air didn't seem to be any hotter and I was frozen. A strong smell of oil and petrol filled the saloon. Just about 2 miles outside Perth, the car lights dimmed quite considerably, the engine would not pull at all and I found that even in first gear the car wouldn't pull. I got out and looked around. At this time of year no one was going about. The bad weather had discouraged them. In 1973, the motorway by-pass linking Perth with the Edinburgh and Glasgow roads had not been built. This meant therefore there were no emergency phones by the roadside. I left on the very dim headlights and set off by foot to find a garage who would help.

At long last I reached civilisation and found a phone box. The phonebook was intact and I was able to call on the services of a local garage. Fortunately, when I told them my story they were able to locate me and together we set off to find the mini. The mechanic who opened the bonnet was amazed. The fan belt had broken and I had travelled some 60 miles with this problem. The mechanic told me my engine had been cooked and I was very lucky that it was still able to operate. I later discovered through other wrestlers that my fan belt been cut by a very irate and humiliated Sid Cooper, who had openly boasted about this to anyone. who would listen. Nice guy eh? Once the repairs had been carried out and the battery recharged

I set off for home yet again. I had been over 7 hours since leaving Dunfermline and I still had 80 miles to travel. By this time my head was splitting, my legs felt like jelly and I had severe pains in my guts. I eventually arrived home at 3.30am. After 3 hours sleep I was up and off to my full time job as if nothing had happened, with the knowledge that at 5.30 that evening I was off again to Elgin to face yet another opponent. I had found it very difficult to concentrate on my work that long Friday, but eventually 5.30 pm came and I was off once again. I soon forgot my poor state of health. The snow had deepened considerably since early that morning and by evening it was treacherous. A more mature head would have said not to go. But I was young and full of confidence in my own abilities. I thought I knew what I was doing. I cannot remember having such a horrific driving experience. Because I had never driven in snow I had to learn the hard way, and believe me this was a hard lesson. The snowfall round the Glens of Found land were always bad but because the mini was so small I could barely see the road ahead. The snowploughs had been out and drivers were advised not to travel unless their journey was absolutely necessary. There were huge dips in the levels of snow, the wind was driving hard, and at times I couldn't distinguish the road from the fields on either side. Suddenly I began to feel very lonely. I didn't, at that time know the road very well so I had no idea how far I had to go. there were slight improvements in patches but on the whole I was extremely worried and wondered if I might become a victim of the severe cold. Some how or other I eventually arrive in Elgin and hurried into the warmth of The City Halls.

I was matched against the experienced veteran, Kevin Connelly. He weighed 12 stone 12 lbs (81.6 kilos) and was 5'7" tall. Normally I dislike these grapplers who use comedy in their bouts. I always feel they are taking the Mickey out of their opponents and belittling them unnecessarily. However, Connelly was a true professional. He was a hard man who used some pretty tough manoeuvres. I suppose I had been hyper when I arrived nearly 2 hours late. I was told I would have to wrestle last. That annoyed me because I knew I would have to face the long journey home again. So, I set about Connelly as if it had been his entire fault. The Irish Liverpudlian pinned me in round 2 and I thought it was the end of the world. However, I battled back and equalised in the very next round. The bout had an abrupt ending when I side stepped an onrush from Connelly and he hit his shoulder off the metal post. He couldn't continue because of the injury and I was awarded the bout. Kevin Connelly was big enough to shake my hand, and praise my ring performance. He took the mike and told the crowd I had real potential and they should consider me a future champion. Praise indeed from the old dog!

Another Scots wrestler who spoke to me for the first time that evening was Bill Ross. Previously he had ignored me when appearing on the same bills. Some years earlier I had written to Bill asking him to train me for wrestling. He never replied. Now here he was telling me what a good grappler I was and offering to give me some tips. We were to become good friends and beat some of the best tag teams around in later years. It a funny old world isn't it? I had my shower, changed into my tracksuit and the set off once again to face the brutal weather. Oddly enough, in the late evening, this was around 11.00pm, the weather had calmed down and the long journey home was at least bearable. I never drove above 30 miles an hours but at least I got home in one piece and lived to wrestle another day. I arrive home about 2.30am. I had a mug of cocoa but I couldn't sleep. The events of the past 2 days had been very traumatic as well as quite brilliant for me in the ring. I had beaten 2 very experienced and much heavier grapplers than myself. I knew I was getting there. The final episode of this saga came with the postman on Saturday morning. He delivered the bill for my car repairs. That was my 2 nights wrestling money gone in one fell swoop. never mind I did have a jolly good Christmas!

At the beginning of the 20th century, a grappler called Farmer Burns, the trainer of the former world heavyweight champion, Frank Gotch, brought wrestling back to popularity by revising the rules of catch -as - Catch can. This style meant a man could be defeated if his shoulders were held down simultaneously for a count of 3 seconds. (A method previously used around the Lancashire area many years before!) An opponent could of course be beaten by submissions, which were taken from the Japanese judo masters, where they were in extreme pain from a hold or lock with no way of escaping, or by being knocked out. This was called American- catch style. Later it was to be renamed All-In, quite incorrectly. Although this style and subsequent rules, were used here in Britain, no one controlled the interpretation of these rules. As a result, different referees and indeed the promoters, operated their own version of the rules and regulations for each contest which varied on every occasion.

It was not until Lord Mount Evans, and a house of commons committee containing the writer Commander Campbell and Maurice Webb M.P., produced a code of conduct in 1948 which was universally agreed by the promoters in Britain, that the rules and regulations became standard throughout the country as a whole. The committee also instituted a series of championship belts to bring order to what had been a very chaotic sport. These have remained almost unchanged since those days, although referees are much more ready to accept following up of moves when opponents are in the prone position if it is considered part of the same, or follow-up move. Similarly, they allow the use of ariel moves off the ropes and corner posts, something quite unheard of in 1948!

In those times people paid for their wrestlers like they paid for their butcher meat. The bigger the bloke, the more money the promoters charged the public, and the more the heavyweight was paid. It was people like the legendary George Kidd, New cross tearaway, Mick McManus, bombastic Jackie Pallo, Eddie Capelli and Ken Joyce, who trail blazed the way for lighter men. They showed the public a new skilful and scientific kind of grappling. Here were muscular yet lighter men, who moved a great speed displaying a vast array of fresh and exciting moves. The holds and counters were very skilful and much more enjoyable to watch. But all that took time. I remember one of the promoters telling me that Jackie Pallo lost every bout in his first 5 years of wrestling, mainly because he had to tackle much heavier opponents. However, as time went on more and more younger and lighter guys got involved and thrilled the crowds with their fast clever moves at lightening speeds. Europe was very keen on these lighter weights, but America, still to this day, prefers the heavies.

Unfortunately, the Lord Mount Evans Committee did not have the necessary authority to impose its will on all the wrestling promoters. Some ignored the new organisation and kept their own champions who laid claim to everything! However, in 1952 Jack and John Dale, along with a friend Les Martin formed the Joint Promotions Ltd. They invited the larger promoters to link with them. People like George De Relwyskow and Arthur Green, the partnership of Norman Morrell, himself a former Olympic champion and Ted Beresford, along with the Dale- Martin team were soon working in conjunction with each other to promote around 40 bills each week throughout Great Britain. By 1955, most of the top professional wrestlers had joined with the new organisation, allowing people the length and breadth of the country to see there favourite heroes and villains.

It was in 1955 that independent television began its famous 4.0pm slot of weekly grappling, this lasted for 33 years. A remarkable run. Longer than any other television programme, with the exception of "Coronation Street!" And maybe "Top of the Pops!" By the sixties the lightweight, welterweight and middleweights were the preferred contests by the public. The lighter wrestlers are far more mobile and tactically aware. The days when 2 large heavy weights spent much of each round holding on to a move in a desperate attempt to squeeze the opponent into submission, are long gone.

By the time I began wrestling for money in the 70's there was a large contingent of speed technicians. George Kidd, Mick McManus, Jackie Pallo & Alan Colbeck were still around, but a new breed was making their mark. People like Vic Faulkner, Bert Royal, Adrian Street, Alan Miquet, Jon and Peter Cortez, Brian Maxine, Johnny Saint, Zoltan Boschic, Mark Rocco, Marty Jones and Jim Breaks. There was never any shortage of talent and the U.K. seemed to lead the way. We held 6 out of the seven European titles, 3 Commonwealth Titles and 2 World Titles. Interestingly enough, the World Title holders were both 2 of the longest reigning champions. George Kidd held the world lightweight title for 26 years, and Mike Marino held the Mid Heavyweight crown for 15 years. Both were outstanding grapplers and a credit to the sport.

I first met Mike Marino when he came to Aberdeen on the first bill I ever wrestled on. He was every inch a champion. He regaled me with stories of what things were like when he first started grappling. Mike Marino believed in the classic style of wrestling and until the day he died, through a blow in the ring, he never compromised on that. No gimmicks, No playing to the gallery, No fancy gowns, Just pure freestyle wrestling. Some wrestlers have a great ring presence. Jon Cortez, Jackie Pallo, McManus, George Kidd, Pete Roberts, Marty Jones. They all had it. But the one who new more than most was the inimitable Mike Marino. Born in London from Italian extraction he was a perfectionist and a quality performer. He was the golden boy pin up of the 1960's but was still wrestling, and still a champion into the 1980's. Following a spell of boxing in the 1950's in France, Marino decided to try tried his luck in Britain, but could not get a licence So he moved into amateur wrestling at the Foresters Club in South London. Moving into the paid ranks he became a crowd puller. He toured the world and learned many skilful moves. He was the first wrestler to appear on ITV in 1955 when the grappling first hit our screens. Although weighing only 14.5 stones, (92 Kilos) Marino's skill and flair lead him to demolish many big continental names. He won the world mid heavyweight title defeating the Greek Mike Demitre in Aberdeen Music Hall.

In his quieter moments Marino continued to work on his classic style, which kept him at the top of his profession until his untimely death following a blow in the ring. He passed on many tips to younger stars and I had many long and useful conversations with Mike. He was a true wrestler's wrestler. He carried himself well, looked well, spoke up for the sport, and behaved in a manner befitting a world champion. Something necessary in any sport. He became known as Mister Wrestling and he well deserved it.

No British book on wrestling would be considered complete without the mention of Bert Assirati. I first heard about Assirati when talking to an old grappler called Sir Athol Oakley. I met Athol in Wales in 1973 when I bought a copy of his book "Blue Blood On the Mat" from him: Athol signed it for me. He recalled many ring exploits of Bert Assirati as did Mike Marino who had had some powerful contest with the great man. Bert Assirati was a powerhouse of a man who literally smashed up other heavyweights in the ring. During the 1950's some grapplers even got together to try to have him banned- such was his ferocity. Bert was not tall for a heavyweight. He was around 5'9" and weighed Had a 19 ¼" neck, and boasted a 53" chest. His strong man feats are legendary, the best known being when he lifted a London black taxi from the front. Like Marino he was a London Based Italian, like Marino he did not believe in gimmicks or sham wrestling which was prevalent in the game during the 1940' & 50s. He asked no favours and expected none. In the early 1903's Assirati went to America and took on both former world champions beating them with such ease, that the minders for the World Champ Jim Londos though it advisable the two mean did not meet since it would undoubtedly have resulted in a win for Assirati. It is testament to his greatness that in over 7000 bouts he was only beaten twice and both of those losses were avenged. Marino described to me the bout in which he took on Frank Sexton a former World heavyweight champion. During the brutal contest Sexton broke Assirati arm. Far form finishing the bout, it simply made him angry! Despite hitting Assirati's body with everything but the kitchen sink, Bert still stood large as life and battling onward. After an hour the bout was declared a draw. He took on the best in Europe and the World at large without a second thought and came through smiling every time. He was indeed a brilliant Heavyweight. The kind of things legends are made of. What a pity I never saw him in action.

In the late 1960's we could boast of nearly 600 wrestlers up and down the country in those days. Some were full time, others were more cautious. One of my heroes was Clayton Thompson who, as well as having a vast range of moves, often copied the technical moves of the great George Kidd. He told me that he turned professional one week and broke his leg the following week. That kept him out of the ring for nearly 6 months. There was, and still is, no insurance company who are willing to insure grapplers against injuries and the promoters didn't pay if you didn't work. So you can imagine how hard it was to survive then. Clayton Thomson was a real classic grappler though other Scottish grapplers saw him as aloof and conceited. I suspect this was because Clay lived in England unlike them. But Thomson was natural in his ring craft. Clay Thomson stands out in my memory as a participant in one of the most scientific bouts I have ever seen. He fought Bert Royal who was the British middle weight champion at the time. It was a nip and tuck battle with move matching move and counter holds coming thick and fast. Both men were extremely fit and it was a brilliant bout to see. Thomson ran out the winner taking the Middleweight crown with him. He well deserved it. Clay was the only British wrestler to hold 5 titles at the same time. He could almost shed or gain weight at will, and kept himself in the peak of conditioning. He often helped coach in the amateur ranks, and did a lot to encourage youngsters to get into wrestling.

The promoters had a wealth of talent at their disposal but sadly they never fully used it. They were not caring employers. They often argued over trivial sums of money needed for travelling, they didn't look after the guys who picked up serious injuries (unless you were one of their favourites) and they kept payments down to a bare minimum.

In the halcyon days of British grappling, I remember being told that they would fly men like Jackie Pallo or Mick McManus up to Aberdeen for one bout against someone like George Kidd. This cost a fortune but must have paid the promoters to do it. By the same token I recall a story from George Kidd telling me that when he first appeared on television he received the sum of £40. Quite a large sum in the 50's. However, that was exactly the same as I received for my first bout in 1976. The money from the television people had gone up, but the promoters kept it the same for the grapplers. In the U.K. there was something like 15 million viewers watching their favourites every week. If the grapplers had been given a percentage of that, they would all have been very rich indeed! One wrestling star, Gentleman Jim Lewis, who entered the ring with a batman, mirror and comb, then proceeded to annoy the crowd by spending ages combing his golden locks, did try to start a union for wrestlers. But such was the wrath of the promoters, he was frozen out and found no promoter booking him. The result left him in need of money and a home in which to live. It wasn't all glamour and glory.

During the early Seventies, when long hair and flared trousers were all the fashion, and I have to admit I was no different from the rest, I continued to conquer all before me. It was April of 1974 when I first fought in my hometown of Aberdeen. I remember climbing the Music Hall stairway heading towards the ring remembering how, as a boy, I had dreamed my dream of becoming a wrestler. My opponent was Alan Bardouville. He was a coloured star from Manchester. Alan was heavily into body building and health foods. He had been a member of the famous Eldorado All Stars and was popular with the crowds. I can't remember much about our contest, except that is was very fair, fast and full of action. I won the contest on a technical knockout when one of my throws resulted in a dislocated shoulder for Bardouville. The crowd enjoyed the bout and Bardouville had no hard feelings. Many grapplers would have refused the verdict, but in the exuberance of youth, I felt I had earned it and wanted it recorded in the record books.

This was the pattern for the rest of that year and much of the next. I travelled around the Country gaining experience and beating more grapplers than I ever lost to. Throughout the summer months I went to every Gala or Games Day where there was wrestling. I ask for my name to be placed on the promoters register to be used as a substitute whenever some one would fail to appear. I was gaining experience and a reputation to match. Then one day late March 76, George De Relwyskow told me he wanted me to appear on Television. I could hardly believe my luck, and accepted only too willingly. It was the Scotland V England football match, which was to be shown live on World of Sport. So, promoter George De Relwyskow had decided to run a Scotland V England tournament. Unfortunately, it proved to me that despite everything, there IS also politics in sport.

I received a letter through the post from Promoter George De Relwyskow telling me that I was to appear on TV in a bout from Sheffield Town Hall. In the 1950's and early 1960's many of the Televised bouts were shown "live" and very often fans never knew who the winner of a particular bout was. However new technology allowed them to pre record bouts and show them later. My bout was to be filmed on a Wednesday evening from Sheffield and shown the following Saturday. It was a Scotland v. England tournament, which were so popular r with the fans. The other 2 wrestlers from Scotland who travelled with me were Bill Ross and "craggy" Tom Dowie. Dowie was a real gentleman. His rough craggy face made home look older than his years, but a fairer man you'd be pushed to find. I picked them up after leaving Aberdeen at 8 am that morning.

Following a very long journey we stopped for a meal at a motorway service station and arrived at Sheffield Town Hall at around 5.30pm. In those days the TV Company insisted that wrestlers were at the hall at least an hour prior to the kick off. This allowed time to be examined by a doctor and time to warm up. I well remember Zoltan Boschic trying to sell me some cuff-links. A nice little sideline of his. He must have been good at it though as I bought 3 pairs of gold cuff links with red ruby imitation jewels in the centre. Well it was the height of the glam rock era!

The show began at 7.30pm prompt. First up was Tom Dowie. He was facing a much lighter opponent in Kung Fu (Eddie Hamill from Ireland) It was a good bout but Tom's knock'em down and drag 'em out style was frustrated by Eddie's cleaver skilful style and poor tom was sent out by the referee for an early shower. Bill Ross was next in. He faced the stylist Vic Faulkner brother of Bert Royal and a very popular wrestler. The contest was one for the true grappling fans. It ended in a drawn contest. One lost and one drawn. The honour of Scotland was down to me now. I entered the ring to loud cheers. It seemed strange people from England cheering for me, using my name, when I had never been this far south wrestling before. However, this was explained by the entrance of my opponent, "cry-baby" Jim Breaks. He was a very accomplished grappler who knew every hold in the book. He had now adopted a rule benders approach to add hardness to his style. This was the first time I had ever faced Breaks.

The bell rang and he launched himself at me. His breath was taken away when I countered his on rushes with fast head throws. It was popular with the fans who began shouting my name even louder. It was great and until then I was enjoying myself. Trading holds and counters with one of the best in Europe and coming off best. It all came to a head in round 4 when I tricked breaks, nipped between his legs and pinned him. I raise my hand in victory. I thought that that was it. I grabbed my tartan towel threw it over my neck and ducked between the ropes.

The fall was announced and George Relwyskow gestured to me to get back inside the ring and carry on. I was puzzled. All the bouts for the tourney had been one fall. Had Relwyskow got it wrong? I tried explaining to the referee and to Relwyskow but Breaks, ever the professional, continued the bout. Seizing the initiative and aware of the confusion he grabbed my wrist, twisted it inside and under my arm, lifting me high into the air. The pain was excruciating and I submitted. I was confused, Angry and I lost it. I had forgotten the golden rule of George Kidd-"the man who keeps his cool, wins the bout." The bell for the final round 6 rang and Breaks tore into me. I resisted for a while and threw him several times but my mind wasn't on it. I was still trying to work out why we were battling against each other when I had taken the only fall. At that point Breaks seized my injured wrist and wrenched another submission from me. He had won the bout by two submissions to one fall. It was later explained to me that the contest had been so good with the fans; the TV director had told Relwyskow to keep it going. The irony was that because my concentration had been broken the last two rounds were not as good as the beginning of the bout. I was furious. I had agreed a one fall contest and it had been changed, not by the promoter, but by the TV people who had thought this would be great viewing. I was so angry. When a fan climbed into the ring and gave Jim Breaks a very large intimation n baby's dummy I grabbed it and smashed it over his head. No doubt the TV people enjoyed that too!! But I had been sickened. I had come along way, played fair, and been beaten by TV cameras. Relwyskow didn't support me although he did sympathise.

I decided that from that day on I would never wrestle in front of the TV cameras again – and I never did. We had a good journey home leaving Sheffield at 9.30pm and getting into Aberdeen at 6.0am after dropping off Tom Dowie at East haven outside Dundee, and Bill Ross at Cullerlie Estate.

I had a similar experience 14 years later when at a European Games Tournament for Special Olympics Held in Glasgow; the TV cameras insisted that the athletics programme be shifted from an afternoon competition to an evening tournament. It upset many of the athletes who had disabilities and were not expecting to run late into the night. But this was the behest of the TV directors. The upside was that they told me if it was done this way the special Olympians would get prime time TV coverage whereas afternoon competitions would be lost to a smaller audience. They clearly had a point. But I don't like being dictated to by people who have never taken part in a competitive sport, and have no idea what the effects of their demands were on the young athletes. But there you are. No matter how much we all don't want it- there is clearly too much politics in sport.

A CHANGE OF MASTER! Joint Promotions had held sway over the bulk of the British wrestlers for about 25 years. I regret to say, that the payment for some pretty good grappling contests never seemed to be reflected in the money the wrestlers received. There was loads of discontent around with Joint Promotions and it came to a head when about the mid seventies, Max Crabtree, George Kidd and Jackie Pallo decided to break with Joint Promotion and form their own Company. Max had been a wrestler himself and had introduced many bright young stars into the business. He was one of the first promoters to bring the big foreign stars into this country. He had an eye for a good match and could fill a hall easily.

During the miners strike and the three day week which happened under the Edward Heath Tory Government, Max still continued to run wrestling through out the North of England and Scotland. He had persuaded some big names to wrestle for him like Adrian Street, Kendo Nagasaki, Albert 'Rocky' Wall, the then British Heavyweight Champion, and also the horse jumping star, Harvey Smith. Smith had always had a love of wrestling. He was a tough customer and put everything into his ring battles. Virtually unknown at that time was Shirley Crabtree, yet to find fame as 'Big Daddy.' The main referee was Max Crabtree's younger brother Brian. He was fit and enthusiastic, quite different from the usual run-of-the-mill refs.

Some of the best grappling was seen round the U.K. at that time as Joint Promotion struggled to keep there stars and as other promoters found success. At one point I was wrestling for both Joint Promotions and Max Crabtree, until George De Relwyskow decided to drop me from his stable. He said," I will be sorry to lose you but you can't work for rival promoters." I was disappointed at this, particularly as Joint Promotions still held the television contract. But at the end of the day Crabtree was providing me with more bouts round the country.

On occasions Max used me as a referee. I never really enjoyed this job, but it did give me front line experience watching the bouts actually happening in the ring. Max ran summer promotions in Aberdeen in the then Palace Ballroom.

This particular evening I had come to watch. During the course of the first contest Brian Crabtree was hurt when the two grapplers collided with him. Brian had to be carried off and taken to the Aberdeen Royal Infirmary. Max was desperate for a referee. That's when he asks me to do the job for him. I had a baptism of fire having to referee a heavyweight clash between Giant Haystacks and the Yorkshire miner "Mucky" Mal Kirk. Haystacks was a very very large man. He measured 6feet 11 inches in his stocking soles. He was a thoroughly unpleasant person and seemed to dislike everyone. He weighed some 32 stone. Mal Kirk on the other hand had been a formidable force in the rugby field and, despite being a rough diamond, was a nice guy outside the ring and a great singer to boot! He was 5'11" and weighed 18 stone. Together they weighed nearly 5 times my weight.

My memory of that bout was when the Giant raced across the ring in a desperate bid to grab Kirk by the throat, and one his way he tramped upon my foot. I crippled around for 6 weeks later! The only other memorable thing about that evening for me, came later when in the changing room Luke McMaster or Martin Rune, (as the Giant Haystacks was known, he had various names and no one ever really knew what his real name was!) he said to me, "If I don't get a woman tonight Ironside, I'm going to use you're ass!" I promptly replied," You'll have to catch me first." He never did thank goodness!!

I went on to alternate between grappling and refereeing during that summer. At the Kelvin Hall Glasgow, I disqualified Mick McManus in a bout with Ed 'Kung Fu' Hammill, the Irish star, and allowed Andy Robbins a long count against Wild Angus (Frank Hoy) to allow Andy sufficient time to get back into the match and apply his famous Powerlock hold. I never said I was unbiased! Andy Robbin was a Scottish hero. When weighing only 14 stones (88 Kilos) he made his mane jumping into the ring and challenging the top heavyweights of the day. What made his name was he subsequently beat them, often using the powerlock. This was a move Andy had learned from a wise old Indian Chief during his tour of Canada, where he won the Commonwealth Mid-Heavyweight Title. Andy once told me," The Chief must have been nearly 90 years of age, but he was still as supple as a monkey. Robbins would travel round the halls offering £1000 to anyone who could break his Powerlock move. There were many takers but no-one ever succeeded.

I have picked up many injuries in the grappling game, but the only one I ever sustained as a referee was in Aberdeen when I was the middle man between Big Daddy and a very Large Yorkshire man known to me as Gordon, and wrestling under the name of The Farmers Boy. He seemed to think my instructions could be ignored because I was quite little in comparison to him. I ran through his legs, jumped up on his back, and even pulled his beard in order to insist on him breaking illegal holds. However, my downfall came when he tore off the padding covering the corner post in order to give Big Daddy a severe case of backache. I noticed him doing this and rushed to the corner to repair the damage. I turned round only to see the 25 stone ((158 kilos) of Shirley Crabtree hurtling towards me. I woke up 30 minutes later in the Royal Infirmary with nurses who brought me round. Apparently, I had cushioned Big Shirley's back and he went on to win the bout. I have to say, that was of little consolation to me. I gave up refereeing after this!

Towards the end of the Seventies Joint Promotions accepted defeat and invited Max Crabtree, the largest independent promoter to join them. Sadly it meant Max leaving Scotland and the North of England and going to work from London. Although he had access to some of the biggest names now, he never had the same success. Part of this was due to him not having to try so hard to survive, and partly with his obsession of making Big Daddy, Shirley Crabtree, a popular figure with the children and the mums and dads. Unfortunately, that in turn, was to lead to the destruction of wrestling in this Country. But more about that later.

One of my last few bouts with Joint Promotions was for Max Crabtree in Aviemore. On the Tuesday night I had wrestled in Aberdeen as had two heavyweights, Honey Boy Zimba and Chief Billy White Cloud. Both of these guys were real gentlemen who did everything with the minimum of fuss and bother. They stayed overnight in the City and in the afternoon I collected them and drove them up to Aviemore. The drive from Aberdeen to Aviemore is quite bleak in that there are long stretches of nothing but open moorland. It was during one of these spells I witnessed something really unusual. Honey Boy Zimba had been fast asleep in the back of my car for most of the journey. The coloured star loved to catch up on his sleep. In the passenger seat beside me was the genuine red Indian Chief. We came on a stretch of road which was blocked due to a very large cow standing on the road, eating the grass off the verges. White Cloud got very excited and started gibbering. He was very concerned that we might be late in arriving at the hall, and he would not have enough time to do a spot of training. He created so much of a noise that he wakened up Zimba. "What the hell's the matter?" Zimba roared. I explained the situation to him. "Holy Mollie!" he grunted. And with that, Honey Boy got out of the car, placed his arms round the neck of the cow, and dragged the poor beast off the road and into the verge. He did this as if he were a little pussy cat. Having so done, Honey Boy stepped back into the car and resumed his kip in the back seat! Now that what I call heavy.

On arrival at the Cinema ballroom in Aviemore I had to share a dressing room with two other heavyweights grapplers, Lee Sharron and Big Jim Moran who was called "Gargantua." Both these guys had a strong dislike for Andy Robbins and as it happened that evening Gargantua was to face Robbins in a Boxer versus Wrestler match. As we were all getting changed into our wrestling gear, I saw Lee Sharron helping Gargantua insert a horseshoe inside one of his boxing gloves. Now Big Jim was known as Gargantua because he was 6 foot 9inches tall and weighed some 27 stone. He would at that size and weight already pack a powerful punch, but with an object like a horseshoe I felt he would seriously damage Andy Robbins. Once changed I raced through to Andy's dressing room to tell him what I saw.

Believe it or not, Andy just laughed. He felt that if Gargantua needed such an instrument to assist him, then he must be running scared. I followed the contest with great interest. Andy always loved to mix it rather than wrestle and he was clearly enjoying this. He won by a K.O. in round 5.

Andy had such incredible strength for a man of his size, in fact he used to train with weights, which were heavier than the British

Weightlifting records at that time. He had a belief in himself that would move mountains. On this occasion, he clearly did. I won my bout that evening against Bobby Ryan and it was one of the most memorable contests I had. Ryan always gave value for money and was one of the cleverest lightweights around. Unfortunately it was my last for Max Crabtree.

Scotland, and the North of England was now without a mainstream wrestling promoter. But comes the hour, comes the man, as they say. Brian Dixon had been a wrestling fan all his life. From Liverpool, Brian had done everything from selling programmes to staging some shows around his hometown. He had been looking to enlarge his "All Star Wrestling Promotions and saw an opportunity when Crabtree returned to what was left of Joint Promotions. Brian had years of experience in the wrestling game, never having grappled himself, but he knew all there was to know about the wrestlers themselves. He could make a keen match and he knew what the public wanted to see. He staged a show at the Music Hall, Aberdeen in 1977.

I went along and introduced myself, along with Bill Ross, who was now living and working as a Gamekeeper in the Park estates in Drumoak, just outside Aberdeen. Brian had heard about both of us and signed us up immediately. I now considered I had a new grappling boss and that's when my tag-team partnership with Bill Ross began. we were to have many successes in the ring, beating such established teams as Hells Angels, Adrian Street and Bobby Barnes, Black Diamonds, Abe Ginsburg and Eric Cutler, and of course the Fabulous Royals, Bert Royal and Vic Faulkner.

We had only 3 years together as a team. Bill was determined to give up wrestling when he reached his 40th birthday. To his credit he did just that, but not before we had one or two adventures together. Bill Ross had been one of the smartest wrestlers to come out of Scotland. He was born in Auchterarder and had lived most of his life around there. He had been a schoolboy friend of Andy Robbins and the knew each other very well. Both had competed in the highland games circuits. Andy at the strength events, tossing the caber, putting the shot etc and Bill at the athletics. Both had been involved in the games wrestling, along with their close friend, Jim Bell. Andy Robbin enjoyed the Cumberland and Westmoreland style of grappling where the participants grasp their arms around each others chests. To win this you have to unsettle your opponent and drop him to the ground, mainly this is done by lifting your opponent off his feet. Whilst Bill also joined in this style, he was more successful at the catch -as-catch can. This is more like amateur wrestling and starts from the recognised referees hold. Auchterarder's Bill Ross was a gentleman of the ring. He was easy going, pleasant, and behaved like the champion he was. Bill had considerable success in the Highland Games circuits both as a wrestler and on the track and field events. Trained by Jim Bell, who incidentally also trained Andy Robbins, Bill had natural ability and excelled at most sports.

In 1970 Bill captured the Commonwealth Lightweight Title form Al Miquet in a fast scientific contest. Then in 1972 he stepped up to take the European Lightweight title from none other than Jim Breaks at the Nottingham Ice Rink. A bout the crowd considered to be a classic. In 1975 he took the world middleweight title off Adrian Street in a hard fought contest. Bill and I teamed up for what turned out to be only 3 years. But in that time we beat the best. I was so disappointed when in 1980 he announced his retrial from the ring. I continued where Bill left off in a series of cracking contest against the Welshmen Adrian Street. We even went to the Shetland Isles to take each other on. A great bout but unfortunately ended in round 5 when Street was disqualified. So much enjoyed was our bout that it took the Shetlanders 3 days partying before I was able to catch a plane home! The drink was flowing and no one seemed to be concerned about getting back to work. I have no idea when Street got off the island.

Both Andy Robbin and Bill Ross had wrestled for Joint Promotions and they had been around the halls since the late 1960's. Bill had picked up the Commonwealth Lightweight Championship and had tried to beat Jim Breaks for the lightweight title of Great Britain. This contest which was held in Nottingham Ice Rink was widely regarded as one of the all time classics. Neither wrestler broke a rule and both were still standing shoulder to shoulder after having given their all. The whole match lasted for 50 minutes and both wrestlers having gained a fall a piece, the result was a drawn contest.

On that same bill, Andy Robbin had been wrestling Albert Rocky Wall for the British Heavyweight championship. But Andy, who liked to rough it up, more than he liked technical wrestling was sent off in disgrace when he applied the Powerlock hold to the champion, gained the submission, then refused to release the hold. He always loved to hold it on just a little bit longer than necessary in order to give his opponents a little more pain! But in a title fight the referee was very strict and rightly so, disqualifying Robbins for his efforts. Robbins was a great fighter. He took part in many memorable contests. He was exciting to watch and very fast for a heavyweight. The only person to ever really handle Robbins was the massive Georges Gordienko. The grappler Georges Gordienko was 5feet 11 inches in height weighed 20 stone and had legs like tree trunks! He was born in Canada of Russian extraction and Georges had one of the fiercest reputations in world wrestling.

On one of the occasions when Relwyskow had taken me back to Leeds with him I witnessed a strange event. I often used to return with the promoter for a week long series of bouts in the North of England. they used a mini bus to transport the "stars" around. However, this time only 3 people were going back and they used a minibus. Gordienko sat at the back pressed hard against the door. Because of the long journey which carried on through the night, we often stopped at the road side all night cafes. Just outside Carlyle we stopped for a snack. Once we had finished we all piled into the van. Geordienko took up his usual position at the back door. Minutes later we were tearing down the motorway. Unfortunately, whoever closed the back door of the van had not done so properly. With the bulk of Georges leaning against it, the door suddenly burst open. Georges fell out, the van screeched to a halt, and I witnessed Georges rolling over in a summersault seven times before picking himself up, dusting himself off, and climbing back into the van as if nothing had happened. How he survived that at such a speed I'll never know. But I tell you that really is being tough!

Gordienko versus Andy was yet another occasion where Robbins was sent off but this time for his persistent refusal to release holds. I suspect that was because he was making little headway with the 20 stone (126 Kilos) master grappler and Robbins decided to simply save face by being sent out. The contest went only 3 rounds. I would have very much liked to see a return bout, but it never happened.

Despite this blot on his record, Andy Robbins traded hold with the best of them and seldom lost. He beat class wrestlers like Mike Marino, Wayne Bridges as well as rough houses like Roy' Bull' Davis, the Welsh Champion Gwyn Davis, Big Bruno Elrington, Wild Angus, 'Mucky Mal' Kirk, Big Daddy and Giant Haystacks. Robbins had some epic clashes with the masked star Kendo Nagasaki, both having beaten each other and provided bouts which would have blistered the paint work in the wrestling halls! He had the best record of any British Heavyweight wrestler and should have been the Champion.

However, promoter politics again prevented this. The promoters liked their champions to live in the south of England where the bulk of the wrestling halls were, and where they could be shown regularly on television, and paraded in the halls for the public to see. Andy extended his fame beyond wrestling when he bought and raised the brown bear' Hercules.' Andy would take the bear round the halls and marques to wrestle himself. Many other grapplers described Robbins as being mad. But he made a lot of money from wrestling the bear and from commercial advertising for which the bear was in great demand. He was one of the most popular wrestlers around, he never ducked a challenge and he was totally unpredictable.

He had many adventures outside the grappling game and was always in demand. In fact one of the most heard cries when some wrestler got a little too big for his boots with their opponent, was "get Andy Robbins to sort him out." A great deal larger than life. That was Andy!

There were a lot of great lightweight wrestlers around. They had all become interested in the game much influenced by the legendary George Kidd. Guys like Zoltan Boschic, Johnny Williams, Jon Cortez and Alan Miquet. They were the pin ups of a generation. Apart from Miquet, I had the pleasure to face all of them in the ring and I beat them all. George De Relwyskow gave me those breaks and I grabbed them with both hands, so to speak! I did also get the opportunity to wrestle many good heavier opponents. They were experienced grapplers with over a stone in weight advantage over me, but I still won. There was John Naylor, who was as tough as they come and very well skilled in amateur wrestling. In fact I would go so far as to say one of the most under rated stars of the grappling game. There was Mick McMichael and Jeff Kaye, both of whom were tag team partners who went on to become very successful referees, later in their careers.

But one of the best matches I had was with Tommy Billington from Warrington, who was known as the Dynamite Kid. He had had the benefit of training in the famous Ted Beckley Gymnasium. Tommy was a natural and still the only man I could claim came close to the great George Kidd. We had a fast and furious bout in Aberdeen. It was a fall apiece when I spun Tommy dropping him on to his back, with his arm trapped beneath him. He could not continue and I was declared the winner. I accepted the verdict and challenged him for his European lightweight Title. I was keen and confident after that battle as Tommy had a large reputation and had been felling all before him. Sadly the bout never came off. Tommy relinquished his title because he had put on too much muscle and was unable to scale down to the lightweight division. Several months later he was off to wrestle in America. I couldn't believe how much heavier and muscular he was when I met him again 6 years later.

Tommy had a wrestling cousin called Dave" boy" Smith who later went on to partner him in America as the British Bulldogs tag team. I beat Dave also. He wasn't such a clever wrestler as his cousin, but he dedicated himself to weight training and put on 10 stone in weight. The pairing did well in America but broke up when the W.W.F. circus took off. Tommy didn't like the farce of this showboating and went to try his luck in Japan. Cousin Dave lived for a while in the States. He did return to the Uk for a spell appearing on bills all over the country. But shortly after returning to the states, he passed away. Rumour had it that drugs were involved. Sadly, the Dynamite Kid seriously damaged his back and is a very unhappy man today. Nonetheless he was one of grappling's all time greats. No one can take that away from him.

My last bout for Relwyskow was in Stirling where I beat Bill Ross to win the Scottish Welterweight crown. The only time I ever beat Bill. (We only fought twice and the second time was a draw!) My last contest for Max Crabtree was in Aviemore where I beat the Lightweight Champion of U.K. Bobby Ryan. He was a great little battler and in the Seventies had many great bouts. It is a great pity he sickened of wrestling because he would have been one of the best around in his weight class. New promoter Brian Dixon had been aware of my run of success and told me he would continue to bill me in catch weight contests if I was in agreement. I always preferred wrestling guys bigger and heavier than myself, because it then became much more of a game of chess, pitting my speed and skill against their strength. however, I almost collapsed with surprise when I saw my first contest was against Steve Logan. I remember Steve Logan as the tag team partner of Mick McManus.

Logan had a jutting jaw, powerful barrel chest, and long black shoulder length hair. He only weighed in around 13stone 5 lbs (85 kilos) but always looked so much bigger and heavier. Indeed his powerful forearm smash was so deadly he often tackled full-blown heavyweights to make an even contest. Logan had some legendary battles with his great ring rival Les Kellett. In fact the two men could hardly have been different. Both weighted the same, both measured 5foot 8inches and there the similarities ceased. Les Kellett played the clown in the ring, baffling opponents with his split second timing. He would just step aside and miss the impact of a full forced blow, the momentum of which usually propelled his opponent into the ropes. He staggered around like a punch drunk granddad, but Kellet was a very very hard man. He terrorised his opponents and was totally ruthless. His antics endeared him to the crowd, but Les was the most disliked wrestler around. He kept himself to himself and did as he pleased. The crowds loved him, but his image in the ring would change immediately he left the roped square.

Les's early life had been spent in engineering and it was as an apprentice that he had been introduced to wrestling. At lunch times the lads with this Bradford firm used to push and pull each other about in a boisterous fashion in a game closer to rugby than anything else! Les was spotted by Len Pickard who took him along to join the Thornbury Health and Strength club. It turned out Mr Pickard was an amateur grappler and the clubs trainer in wrestling and weight training. He took to wrestling immediately but when it came to competitions Les was beaten seven bouts on the trot. He gave up heart and left the club. Mr Pickard tried on several occasions to persuade Les to rejoin but he refused. Until one day Pickard virtually frogmarched the 17-year-old Kellet back to the gym and right into the training. Finally, Les became the Yorkshire champion at his weight and there was no going back. Following this Les joined the merchant navy as an engineer. He wanted to see the world- and he did. On his return home he met an old friend Joe Hill who was a grappler now refereeing. After a years intensive training, Les Kellet was introduced to George Relwyskow Snr. Being paid 25 shillings (£1.25) per bout, Les began wrestling twice a week. He was a very hard man. Sadly Les spent his last days in a nursing home but remained a character to the end of his life.

Steve Logan, on the other hand was a real gentleman. He was quiet, unassuming, and would have helped anyone. He was a former Italian speaking army physical training instructor. He was a member of the South London Judo Society but gave it up as he thought it was a bit soft! He boxed regularly for the Fisher Boxing Club and later the Fitzroy Lodge Boxing club, but it was in wrestling he saw his future. Contrary to his tough guy image, Logan was in market research and played the stock market. Steve lived all his life in Brixton. In the ring he was hated by the crowds because of his appearance, but of the two, I much preferred Steve. The famous tag team of McManus and Logan was feared all over Europe. However Steve Logan actually tagged with "iron jaw" Joe Murphy more than Mick McManus. Murphy had been a school boy friend of Logan. But the huge crowds that saw McManus & Logan on TV catapulted their fame in skulduggery. Just shows the power of television! Nonetheless, when seeing myself billed against him, I knew this would be my greatest challenge.

I trained extra hard and learned some new moves and counters. I prepared a game plan and was 200% fit and ready when the contest came round. I climbed into the ring that evening with the cheers of the crowd ringing in my ears. Then I could hardly believe my eyes. As Steve Logan entered the ring he was a tall, handsome, young man weighing 12 stone. Clean cut and very new to the game. This was a different Steve Logan, and yes that was his real name. Poor lad got the full force of my pent up feelings and my punishing training routine. I beat him by 2 straight falls in rounds 3 and 4. He was to go on to become a very clever technical wrestler and brought a lot of credit to the game. It is a great pity he didn't stay around longer. We met twice more in the ring and I won on both occasions, but it was getting harder each time, such was his improvement.

Bill Ross had a much tougher time in his first bout for All Star wrestling promotions, he faced long time rival, Adrian Street. Recognising our crowd appeal, the astute promoter, Brian Dixon paired Ross and me as the Flying Scots Tag Team and together we beat some of the best in the game.

Tag Team wrestling was introduced to bring a different type of excitement to the proceedings. it became so popular there was to have been a tag team title for the Heavyweight Teams and one for the others. However, this never got off the ground because of the breaking up of Joint Promotions. Pity really. There were a number of really good pairings around. Jon Cortez & Alan Miquet; Ted Heath and Alan Dennison; Alan Colbeck and Peter Preston. All great teams who drew large crowds every time they were in action. They had a blend of skill and ruthlessness which got results. Many people thought the Royal Brothers team were the best, but McManus & Logan would have claimed differently. The south London boys were the one team we didn't face but all the others we beat, including the Black Diamonds, the Hells Angels; and Jackie Pallo and his son Jackie Junior.

The Pallos were the easiest mainly because Jackie junior was not very useful. His father had been a great influence on the game and had produced many spectacular and unusual moves. But J.J.had nothing special. He wore the same colourful trunks, sported the long hair complete with the ribbon, but there the similarities ended. I have nothing against J.J. but he was just an average grappler. And, in this game as his father showed, you need to be special to make it to the top. Nonetheless, I enjoyed the clash with Pallo snr, who was very skilful and cunning in the ring. Pallo and his rival McManus had some epic battles. Together they could command an audience of nearly 12 million people when matched on independent television. No one ever forgot their clashes. To this day the pair dislike each other. Unfortunately Pallo was a casualty of the break up of joint promotions. Jackie snr. Went into partnership with Peter Keenan and in some venues Max Crabtree but did most of his promoting in the London Area. Sadly when Crabtree took over he never invited Jackie Pallo back into the fold and a great character was lost to the wider wrestling world.

As a Promoter, Pallo was superb. He never cheated the men and always treated then in the way he wanted to be treated himself. I recall on one occasion the grapplers turned up at the airport to fly off to a wrestling contest, only to be met by Pallo who told them the engagement had been cancelled. However, Pallo paid the guys a flat rate of money so that they wouldn't be out of pocket. I have never known any other promoter be so generous. But that's the kind of guy Jackie Pallo snr was. He treated others as he would expect them to treat himself.

It was late in November when Bill Ross and I beat the American dream and Barry Douglas in Aberdeen. We were delighted with the win because both were heavyweight grapplers. But Bill had not been his usual self. He was now complaining about a pain in his stomach. We were due in Perth next evening so I thought it best to take Bill to the local Hospital for a check up. Bill, stubborn as ever refused saying he would be alright. However, at 6.0pm next evening just before I was due to collect him, Bill phoned to say he had food poisoning and could not wrestle that evening. I set off for. Perth City halls myself. During the course of that evening, I met a young wrestling fan called Frank Cullen. He was 18 years of age, trained with weights, a real enthusiast and determined to become a wrestler. Frank had pestered promoters before but they all gave him the brush off. This particular evening, Brian Dixon was wondering how to organise the programme without Bill to team with me. We were billed to face the Barrons, an experienced team of Steve Peacock and Robby Barron.

After a lot of thought, I persuaded the Promoter to let me go into the tag team with Frank Cullen by my side. Brian wasn't keen. He didn't know how well this young lad could wrestle. The crowd would get angry if they felt he was just a fall guy. Chances were I would get a bruising from the Barrons and Cullen would be of no help to me. Could give the Barrons an easy victory and the Scottish crowd would feel cheated. After great lengthy debate Frank was summoned and I told him the news. He was thoroughly delighted. Naturally he had all his gear with him and changed in double quick time!

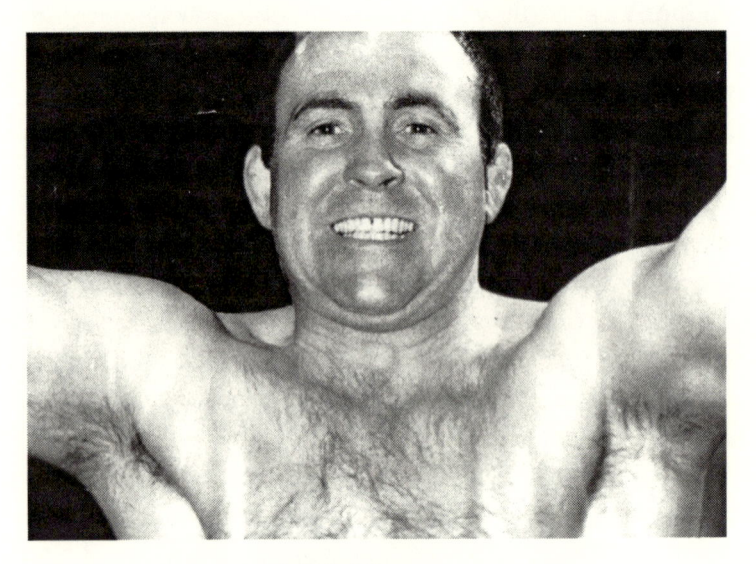

Mick Manus

Unmasking of Kendo Nagasaki

Len Ironside
Scottish Champion

Super Destroyer
Pete Roberts

George Kid 26 year World Champion

Len Ironside Commonwealth Champ

Dynamite Kid Tommy Billington

Frank Cullen: Ironside Ian McKenzie Sandy Thomson

Frank Cullen was wonderful. He showed a great fighting spirit. Despite the fact that Frank got beaten up several times, and was really put through the mill by Peacock and Barron, but Cullen stoutly refused to quit. He tried to help me when we got in trouble and certainly pulled his weight in the team. He actually was badly bruised after this contest, but happy in the knowledge that we had won by the only fall necessary which I gained after 17 minutes. What a baptism of fire. Frank's only wrestling experience at that time was as an amateur when he trained at the Bridge of Allan club in Dunblane. I recall 3 years later, a bout between Terry Jowett and Frank Cullen. It was one of those real" men's" battles. A contest, which had everything. All the other grapplers on the bill left the dressing room to watch it at first hand. What a tremendous scrap it was too. Cullen won Over the much more experienced Jowett. Frank 'Chic' Cullen was to go on to become one of the great Scottish wrestlers and the British Heavy middleweight champion for 4 years, beating such well established names as Marty Jones, Mark "Roller ball" Rocco, and Dave 'Fit' Findlay. Not bad for a lad from the infamous "Raploch" in Stirling.

His only real problem was that he was impulsive. Often he would leave these shores for contests in Germany and the like. Because of this he was regarded as unreliable by some promoters. They consequently stopped booking him as often as they would have liked in case he let them and the crowds down. Pity really because Frank was a very talented grappler. His brief spells in America enhanmced his reputation. In fact I would suggest he was one of the best ever to come out of Scotland. Sadly he was always under rated.

There were many good Scottish grapplers around. They never seemed to be top of the bill material, but they were certainly value for money. Guys like "Craggy" Tom Dowie. He was a very honest and sincere man whom you could depend on in any crisis. But in the roped square he tried to demolish his opponents in double quick time; often incurring the wrath of both the crowd and the referee! He was a jack of all trades and spent most of his time as a fisherman off the coast of Carnoustie. Lee Thomas was also from around the same area. He had the looks and the build for a good light heavyweight, but he tried too much of the George Kidd stuff which didn't really suit him. For a short while he was the tag partner of the great George Kidd and tried to copy the moves of the maestro, but once the partnership broke up he fell into obscurity. I often felt that Tom (his real Name) was more interested in running his pub in Broughty Ferry rather than the hurly burly of wrestling. I mean he loved the glory of appearing with the great George Kidd, but when he had to put in some hard work on his own, he didn't really shape up. I often felt that had he been prepared to work a bit harder, he would have been a star in his won right. Sadly, this never happened. Others like Bob Richardson, Jay Scott, Bruce Welsh, Jock Cameron, Duncan Faichney all had great staying power and considerable skill, but they did not excite the crowds. As a result they never topped the bills.

Apart from Frank "Chic" Cullen another lad from Scotland who came to the ring at that time was Brian MacInallay from Torbrek also in Stirling. He had great potential, which yet again never shone. He enjoyed his wrestling but I have to say it was the wrestling with the ladies at the back door following the bouts at which he excelled most. Those girls known as Ring Rats were all around him and he gave them lots of encouragement and then some. If he had given as much time to the ring grappling he would have been a Scottish champion.

After the break up of the Thomas/Kidd pairing, Max Crabtree along with the retired boxing champion, Peter Keenan, had the inspirational idea to tag the perfectionist Kidd with Roughhouse Andy Robbins for a full 8-month season at the Kelvin Hall in Glasgow. Max Crabtree's instinct as usual, was correct in that the fans loved the team. Two great Scots heroes fighting together, side by side, shoulder to shoulder. The reality however, was very different. There was little love lost between the two Champions. Kidd preferred to remain quiet and concentrated inside the ring. No gimmicks, no playing to the gallery. A skilful artist at work, Andy was the exact opposite. He ruffled feathers, worked up the crowd, argued with referees and behaved in a very loud manner. It was like the pairing of a scientific artist and the street brawler. In fact it was alleged that things got so heated between them, that one evening, having long tired of Robbins school boyish pranks, Kidd produced a loaded revolver and threatened to "blow your fucking brains out" if Robbins didn't stop larking around with him. They have never talked to each other since. The following season in Glasgow Kidd wrestled solo and so did Robbins. Neither having benefited from the tag team experience.

I was doing quite well myself. I appeared at the Caird Hall in Dundee and beat cry Baby Jim Breaks, who was the reigning European Lightweight Champion. Breaks was a very skilful wrestler, but decided to increase his Crowd-pulling capacity by adopting rule-benders attitude.

I recall many years ago in Aberdeen, seeing Breaks face the European Welterweight Champion at the time, Alan Colbeck. The pair produced some classic moves showing hold and counter hold catch grappling at its best. Breaks failed to beat Colbeck that cold evening, but the bout will go down as one of the best of its kind. Seeing Jim Breaks adopt this more aggressive style was a disappointment for me. I think because I felt the public were being robbed of the chance to see a really great technical wrestler. However, in 1976, Breaks had only just beaten me in a televised bout from Sheffield. This was my opportunity to get my own back - and I did. I beat him by 2 falls gained in the 4th and 5th rounds. The crowd went wild. I challenged him for the title and I felt really warm inside that night.

In my early years, when I had travelled to Dundee Railwaymen's Social club, I made many grappling friends. They were a good bunch of lads, dedicated to wrestling and they were only too keen and helpful to me when I was starting off. They knew each other by some strange names like "Pete the Greek" and "Dusty Miller." Some of them were at the Caird Hall that evening. We got talking and they asked me if I would come along to some of their shows that summer to help them out. These guys were full of enthusiasm, but they would never be anything more that average grapplers. They put on a lot of shows for charity in Dundee and raised money for all sorts of good causes. But because there were no stars amongst them, they always had to wrestle each other and the bills always lacked any kind of sparkle.

I introduced Frank Cullen to the lads as he needed to gain some grappling experience, and reunited them with a fellow Dundonian called John Hannah. Hannah had been serving with the air force in Lossiemouth and had done some wrestling jobs for Max Crabtree in

Elgin and Inverness. He was about 5'4" and had at least some wider experience than his colleagues back home in Dundee. I felt these two new lads would help add some new blood into their contests. In this context I also agreed to do some shows for them.

The first bout I did for them was against young Frank Cullen at the Mecca Bingo hall in Dundee. During the interval of the bingo, which usually lasted about 30 minutes, they had a main event to keep peoples attention. Prior to this, during the other shorter intervals, which lasted only 15 minutes other bouts were fought out. Frank gave a good account of himself and the crowd thoroughly enjoyed it. This was a worthy top of the bill contest. However, my name was very well known now in Dundee and I had to be cautious in case any of the large promoters found out about me working for what was technically opposition promoters. Joint Promotions and Brian Dixon were very jealous of what they would see as people muscling in on their stars. So, I had my mother make me a bright yellow mask, bright yellow trunks and black socks. I called myself the "Avenger" and I did 9 more shows for the Dundee lads. It certainly helped with their audience figures.

However, one of my most embarrassing moments comes from that brief spell of wrestling. They had arranged a charity bout in the Caird Park one Sunday afternoon. It was open air and it was free. The Dundonians crowded in! Fortunately, it was a beautiful sunny day. But I took exception at having to walk 300 yards to the clubrooms where we could get changed. I did not want any grass or earth to get on my boots and make them slippery. So, I decided to get changed in the small tent beside the ring, which was to be used for selling drinks and ice creams. I was in the middle of changing, had stripped down to my birthday suit when suddenly a bunch of children who had been hanging around outside, pulled out the tent pegs and the whole structure collapsed in on me. More in anger than fear I rushed outside to find out what was happening only to realise I was providing a wonderful free peep show, with all my manhood on display for the people who were waiting for the wrestling to start! A most moving experience. Wrestling is full of moments to remember and this is one I have never forgotten.

During that spell of my career, I was matched against some of the cream of Europe. I wanted the experience to help me with a proposed assault on the European Championships. Wrestling in Europe was a bit different then. The U.K. held 7 out of the eight Championships of Europe and our grapplers were definitely superior. However, The continentals had unusual styles and I needed to get used to them. The French and Spanish were very Ariel. They would use a lot of high flying manoeuvres off the ropes, off the corner pads, and even off YOU if you let them! The Italians and the Germans were much slower and more traditional in the solid hold and counter hold skills.

In Leeds I wrestled Michael Salnier who is the only grappler who had to look up to me from his 5feet frame. He was fast but came to grief when he jumped off the top ropes and into my chest. I managed to catch him and swung him round with his arm in a back hammer. He submitted immediately and could not continue. He was in a great deal of pain.

Back in the dressing room none of the other wrestlers would talk to me because I had damaged a man littler and lighter than myself. I never did understand this logic because all of my grappling career bigger heavier men have been trying to disable me without any qualms! I think professional jealousy might have had something to do with it. I faced other greats like Albert Sanniez, the Lightweight champion of France, Paco Pastor the Middleweight champion of Spain, and Kadar Hasouni, the Lightweight Champion of Italy. He was memorable because he looked like an angel with gentle facial features like a young girl, but he fought like a tiger. I beat them all convincingly. So much so, that the French promoters, Walter Bordes, and Roger Delaporte who promoted spectacular bills in the Elysee, Monmartre, Paris, took me over to France for a 16 day tour during which I had 10 bouts. I didn't loose any of them, but I have to say I never felt the calibre of opponent was ever as high as our own British stars.

Britain held 7 out of the 8 European titles at that time, and it was not by accident.

Al Miquet has always been a wrestler that I have admired for his sheer skill and guts. He left these shores and was living in France when I met him during that tour. Al Miquet had always made a big impression here in the U.K. (he comes from Huddersfield) and set the tag team scene alight when he teamed up with Jon Cortez to from one of the best teams ever. Regrettably, Bill Ross and I never got to face them. They were both fast lightweights with skill to back it up. However, I felt very proud to be able to meet Miquet who kept himself to himself and never really received the recognition, for his skill, which I believe he deserved. We exchanged stories and experiences that afternoon and discussed our tactics for that evening. I never saw him again.

About this time Max Crabtree contacted me. He was on the lookout for some new talent. He always preferred the heavyweights and wanted to enlist the Highland Games Champion, Bill Anderson who also lives in Aberdeen. Bill was Close to retiring from active competition in the Highland Games, and Crabtree thought this new challenge would spark flame inside Big Bill. I was given the job of contacting Bill and trying to persuade him to participate in wrestling. Bill Anderson had been the most successful Highland Games Heavy of all time. He had a string of records to his credit beginning in 1959 and continuing until 1975. He became interested in athletics at the age of 15 and trained with 100% dedication on his fathers farm in Bucksburn. Bill turned professional at the age of 17 competing at games in Alford, Aberdeenshire. He was a champion in Caber Tossing; Hammer Throwing; Shot putting and had even tried his hand at boxing. Wrestling at the games was his least favoured event. Although, the popularity of Highland Games resulted in many foreign trips to competitions as far a field as Japan and USA to Sweden and Australia.

In one famous incident Bill Anderson defeated a champion Sumo wrestler using the games Cumberland Style. So upset was the Jap he insisted that Anderson wrestle him in his traditional sumo style. Despite the fact that the sumo grappler launched himself at Bill like a Bull at the gallop, Bill stood his ground, didn't flinch, and grappled the Jap to the ground. Needless to say the Japanese gave Bill their total respect. Anderson stands 6 feet 2 inches, weighed something like 20 stones (126.9 kilos) has a 50"chest, 17 inch biceps, and 30-inch thighs.

But the biggest thing about Bill Anderson is his kind manner and honest attitude. He is respected all over the world for his dedication and effort. The ideal ambassador for any sport in any Country. Despite my best efforts, Bill wanted nothing to do with grappling. He was a quiet unassuming gentleman, who had no wish to hurt or harm anyone. For these reasons he said no to Crabtree's offer. It was wrestling's loss. But no one will ever make big Bill Anderson do anything he does not want to do. Bill still lives in Aberdeen and will always be regarded as one of the all time greats.

I have a long time friend called James Knox. He is 6 feet tall and weighs around 14 stones. We have been pals since schooldays. He would have made a great wrestler had he not joined the forces. He had 4 brothers. Like me they enjoyed watching wrestling from an early age and supported me during my ring career. However my mate Jim has only seen me wrestle live once. Once was enough. It was when he was in the Royal Navy stationed in Lossiemouth. He went along to the Elgin Town Hall and was joined by 3 of his brothers Angus, Melvin and Philip. They were quite happy when I came on. I was facing a chap called Steve Peacock. He was a long blonde haired tough nut but his wrestling skills were limited. Not that my friends waited to find that out. At one point Peacock was giving me a bit of a pasting when Jim, Angus and Melvin and Philip jumped the ring and got stuck into Peacock. Of course the referee disqualified me much to my disgrace. So Jim was never invited back!

In 1978 I was to receive 2 stunning shocks. Firstly, after 3 great tag team competitive years, Bill Ross announced he was retiring from wrestling. I couldn't believe it. We had one of the best track records around and Bill was going to pack it in. I tried to persuade him not to leave but his mind was made up. Bill had had one of his classic confrontations with Adrian Street, which ended up with Ross winning the World Middleweight Title off him. Street was so angered by The, as he described it," fluke result," that he set about destroying the belt itself. He was later to receive a three-month ban from grappling and a £500 fine for his actions that evening. However, at that point Ross decided to call it a day. He told me he had always intended to retire from the ring on his 40th birthday. He had no intention of continuing until forced to retire through serious injury.

I admired his decision and the will power he had to stick to it. The fact he had won a major championship simply crowned his career. His final contest in Aberdeen was supposed to have been against Adrian Street, but the ban on Street prevented this contest and Ross accepted a substitute, The American Dream, instead. Bill won and that was the end. I missed him. For me the tag team bouts were over. I did experiment with a few other lads but nothing could match the understanding I had with Bill Ross. I took up the battle against his old adversary Adrian Street. We had several great bouts. Street won one, I won two, and on two other occasions he was disqualified. What a man. Despite looking and dressing like a drag queen he was as tough as they come. He knew how to wrestle as well as mix it. One of our bouts took place in the Shetland Islands. We stayed at opposite ends of the Islands and when our bout had ended (in a disqualification) the Islanders spent two days with me celebrating whilst Street took the first plane home. For me that was a wonderful experience. I haven't drunk so much ever again!!

But give Adrian Street his due, when he was wrestling in a town he would arrive in the morning, dress up in his gear with usually died orange hair, and he would walk the streets of the city shaking hands with people and encouraging them to come along and see him in action. He knew how to promote the game.

Then came shock number 2. The title holder of the Commonwealth Middleweight Championship, Canadian Len Holt retired through injury. The board of control decided that a pool of 32 wrestlers from various Countries throughout the Commonwealth would be matched, in a knock out tournament over 3 months to decide the new champion. Nominations were opened. Although this was 2 weights above my weight, I entered my name.

I stepped up my training routine to cope with this task. Normally I used to do a 5-mile run, three times a week, followed by a 45 minute yoga session; with 70 minutes of weight training every second night. (except Sunday when I took my day of rest!) I never liked running, and to this day, Indian athletes prefer squat training to road running. Something I whole-heartedly agree with. However, in order to boost my cardiovascular system and my leg power, I decided to use the local mountain of Bennachie. It would take a good walker about

60 minutes to reach the summit and return to the start. I filled a back pack with 100 lbs of weights and ran up and down Bennachie twice, three times per week, until the whole routine took me only 50 minutes. Needless to say I reduced the 5 mile runs to 3 mile runs for this duration. It was excellent training and gave me the edge in many long distance bouts. Weights are great for building power and strength; Yoga gives the body elasticity and suppleness; the mountain running gives you an overall heart and lungs capacity for endurance. It was a routine, which stood me in good stead. Fortunately, we are blessed with some beautiful scenery and countryside in the North East of Scotland; there are plenty of good mountains, hills and river walks where concentrated training can be done.

My parents even had a little cottage in the village of Catterline, which I put to good, use. The cottage had no electricity, no running water and an open fire. It was good exercise fetching pails of water from the tap at the foot of our hill, hacking up wood for the fire and living a fairly Spartan existence. I used to do this for 3 full weeks before any important contest. Coupled with my training routine it was great discipline and healthy training. Then came the bombshell, the Board of Control decided, who knows why, that the pool of wrestlers would be reduced to 16 and all 3 wrestlers representing U.K. would come from England, because it was alleged they would be more able to travel at short notice! The truth of the matter was of course, that the Promoters, all based in England, wanted the new champion to come from somewhere which was in easy reach of their largest Halls. I nearly quit on hearing that news. It was the Same selfish attitude of the promoters, which robbed me of my victory on television, and which constantly prevented me facing the champions with their titles on the line. George Kidd, Andy Robbin and Bill Ross had previously had similar problems. Unless you stayed in England within easy reach of their large halls they didn't really want to know. And, as the main promoters were the Board of Control there was no one to appeal to. This has always been the way.

When I look around and see the trash that the Americans are selling on International television for wrestling, I blame that on the U.K. promoters. They never did market the game either at home or abroad. Here we had 7 European Champions, 3 world champions and no promoter ever tried to tell people about it.

In the 1960's there was a regular monthly magazine published called "The Wrestler." It had news and views of all the current grappling stars, details of venues throughout the country, forthcoming bouts which were of interest to the fans, details of the champions in all weight divisions, and human stories about the other side of wrestling. The sport of wrestling attracted people from all walks of life. We had teachers, Doctors, Ministers of Religion, truck drivers, politicians, ballet dancers, comedians, show jumpers, the list is endless. There was a lot to tell and the fans wanted to know. But when the magazine got into difficulties in the early 1970's no promoter would help to bail them out. Despite the fact it was the only National magazine which catered for the wrestling fans. It sold at 25p a copy. I bet the fans would have willingly paid £1.00 a month to keep the magazine on the news racks. But no one helped. This was at the time of the 3 day week and when a gallon of petrol cost 35p. But even at that price the promoters could have sold the magazine around their halls, bought advertising space and given more thought to selling the game. Instead they were only interested in their own local programmes!

When you see the stuff the Americans do, they have wrestling figures, costumes like the wrestlers, confectionary and ice cream products endorsed By the various wrestlers, annuals, bath powder and soap, hats, pictures, virtually everything you can think of. But in Britain the promoter only sold himself and the show, which he happened to be promoting that evening. It was left to some of the top names to do their own thing. For example, Mick Manus endorsed vitamin pills and a German Spring for fitness; Jackie Pallo endorsed vitamin pills; Geoff Portze created a fitness course and sold it with limited support. Some enterprising guys like Adrian Street, would arrive at the town where they were wrestling, dress up in his gear, and walk around the city introducing himself to all who would listen. That certainly helped to sell the seats at the local hall in the evening, but support from the promoter would have been better. So here again was an example of promoters only thinking of themselves.

Despite this set back, I think this episode added a new hard edge to my wrestling style. I faced people like Jeff Kaye, John Naylor and Mick McMichael. All of them were heavier and much more experienced that I was, but I defeated them all. Such was my controlled anger. Then suddenly there was a ray of hope. I was offered a bout in London. On the bill was the newly crowned Commonwealth Middleweight Champion, from Malta, Tony Borg. Something told me I should accept the contest j just to size up Borg. So I took it. As fate would have it, I went on first and beat my opponent Irish John Faye. Then as I was waiting to see the final contest involving Tony Borg, news came through his opponent had been involved in a car crash and couldn't make it. I instantly agreed to wrestle for a second time that evening. The contest was hardly a classic. Mainly Because I was very cautious weighing up my opponent at every opportunity, then suddenly I saw an opportunity and grabbed the only fall of the contest to win the bout. I was ecstatic. They couldn't stop me now. I challenged Tony Borg in front of that crowd for his new title. Borg was only too willing to oblige. He desperately wanted to get his own back. However, when we came to agree the contract, I wanted as the winner of that bout to have the title matched held in my hometown of Aberdeen. But as the T.V. stations were interested, it was arranged for London, mainly for their convenience. It was set for 25th of January, Burns Night. What an omen! Then, yet another blip! Because the T.V. rights were not with Brian Dixon, it could not be televised. Much later in the late 1980's, every large promoter was to get their own top grapplers featured on Saturday afternoon bills, but at the end of the 1970's that privilege still belonged to Dale Martin/Max Crabtree.

Dixon, with only 4 weeks to go before the contest, managed to persuade Tony Borg that as he was known all over the U.K. (Mainly due to the famous tag team pairing of himself and his twin brother Ignatious, the Borg Twins) It would be better to have the contest in Scotland or the North of England, where I was better known. That way the contest would have a bigger crowd appeal. Tony Borg to his credit saw the economic sense of this and signed a fresh contract for the contest to be held in Aberdeen. From this problem had come a better solution which actually favoured me. I couldn't have been more delighted.

It was a cold evening in January 1979 when I stepped into the ring at Aberdeen Music Hall to tackle the very competent Tony Borg. However, I was confident, very fit, and eager to prove myself. It was a fast moving bout with lots of skilful manoeuvres. The crowd loved it. Sadly the end came in round 6 when, although we both had a fall each; I caught Borg coming off the ropes at speed and threw him. As he landed he dislocated his shoulder and could not carry on. The referee was keen to declare the bout a no contest as no one had actually won, the bout being stopped through injury. For some strange reason I agreed. I think I had wanted to show the promoters and the fans that I would have been a better champion. Winning this way did not give me the satisfaction of being in control. reluctantly I agreed the bout be declared a no contest, despite the fact I could have claimed the title, and agreed to meet again. We met in a non-title bout in the Caird Hall, Dundee in February where I won again. When the following month we had our return bout for the title, again in Aberdeen, I convincingly beat Borg, who for some reason became very frustrated at me and lost his temper. I used this opportunity to apply an inverted Irish Whip and drag a scream of pain from Borg as he submitted to the hold. At last I had made it. The Commonwealth Middleweight Champion. The first Scot to hold the title. It was a great night and one I will never forget.

I celebrated by enjoying a meal at a local Chinese Restaurant along with some colleagues. Folk I worked with John Lawrence, Doug McKay, Sylvia McKay, Eileen Davidson, George Laing, Pat Cormack and my mate Billy Ironside.

Billy and I had a great relationship. He wasn't related but came to work in the then called Department of Social Security where I was his manager. I had to train him. We got on very well and became very close. Billy was brilliant at Badminton. He was a champion winning many titles. Had he concentrated in his fitness etc he would have been a world-beater. He had a tremendous smash. The deal was I would teach him to wrestle if he would teach me to play badminton. Well once he taught me to play badminton he decided not to go through with the wrestling part of it. He didn't fancy the strict training regime. Pity really because he was about 5' 4" and solid as a rock. But his love of booze and gambling came before any sport.

I remember taking part in a doubles contest at the Kelvin Hall. On the Saturday we did very well but following a heavy night of drinking on Billy's part we went out in the next round. He was without a doubt the stronger partner; I just made up the numbers. Without his skills the tournament was lost for me. Had it been a wrestling contest rather than badminton contest the result would have been the other way round. Billy was a super guy and I had hoped he might replace Bill Ross as my tag partner but it wasn't to be. Despite our close relationship we drifted apart when Billy left the Department of Social Security and went to work elsewhere and I was elected as a local councillor.

I well recalled the fast and furious tag team action involving the Borg Twins, which I had followed on T.V. What a pity Bill Ross was no longer active. We could have had a great tag-team match against them. An interesting curiosity. Neither Tony Borg nor myself were middleweights when we held this title. The middleweight division is from 11st 11lbs (74 kilos) to 12 stone 8 lbs (79.8 Kilos) We were both lightweights, which is anything up to 11 stone.

The commonwealth Middleweight title had been vacant for several years, following the retirement from the ring of the Canadian Len Holt. It first became a major title in 1951 when it was then known as the British Empire Middleweight title. It was won by Vic Coleman at the Wimbledon Palace. It followed from an open tournament Where Vic Coleman had to defeat such names as Bob Archer O'Brien, Ken Joyce, Eddie Capelli, Jack Dempsey, Mick McManus and George Kidd. All of whom were in their early years gaining experience as they went. Coleman had begun wrestling at the age of 9 years of age training with his father at his Gym. He later became one of the world's youngest grapplers at the tender age of 15. He was a well-respected wrestler in whose shoes many would want to follow. I felt extremely proud that I had been the first Scot to win the title.

In other combat sports like boxing, after the elation of actually winning a title wears off, you then begin to plan for next and bigger pay days. Not so in wrestling. You are only as good as your last bout. You still need to work at becoming better known. It is a fact that the best paid grapplers were not always the Champions. I always recall the first words Max Crabtree said to me after my very first bout."

Kid you've got to make an impression. Doesn't matter if they (the crowd) love you or hate you; they've got to remember you."Hence the reason that well established grapplers like Mick McManus and Pallo spent the largest part of their careers keeping their names in the news and aggravating the crowd. People often came to see if they would be beaten by the latest hopeful, or the current Champion in another weight division. They did both eventually become champions in the 70's; McManus after beating Vic Faulkner for the European Middleweight Title, and I hasten to say, without breaking any rules. And Jackie Pallo, for a short while, after defeating Bert Royal for the cruiserweight title. But they were well established stars before this.

Conversely, Alan Sergeant the British Welterweight Champion, Alan Colbeck the European Welterweight Champion, were never great crowd pullers despite both being very competent champions. They had to be matched against someone who could bring out the best in either of them to draw a crowd. Don't misunderstand me, both were dour earthy grapplers but they couldn't pull in the crowds by themselves. Just an illustration of the contrasts between styles and public acceptability. This was one of the reasons why a number of competent wrestlers like Reg Trood, Len Hurst, Pat Roach and many more became known as "cannon fodder." They would put up a great battle against the top men around, but they were never going to pull in a crowd on their own. In fact Pat Roach, or" Roachie" as he was known in the business, never really came into his own until all the great heavies retired. He had no real personality in the ring and is best remembered for a bit part in the T.V. show "Aufwiedersien Pet." He was a very nice gentleman despite that.

People like Adrian Street, Zoltan Boschic, Brian Maxine, Steve Haggarty, Wild Angus etc, recognised the need to keep their names in the publics minds and tried to make themselves known, in other ways. In fact this became more important than actually winning a title for some of them. It always was a bone of contention seeing the boxers make big money whilst the grapplers, who trained much harder and were more versatile athletes never had the earning power. Promoters kept that for themselves. Wrestling is a sweet life while it lasts. But it doesn't last very long. And, if you take it up in order to get rich, you will be greatly disappointed! Despite that, I still believe it's the greatest game in the world.

There are many reasons why grapplers decide to hide their faces behind a mask. Some want to conceal their true identity because they would be frowned upon in their profession. Others because they were probably just plain ugly! There were only a handful of really good masked men. These were the ones who could win bout after bout without ever loosing. The rule in U.K. was absolutely clear. If a masked man lost his contest, he had to remove his mask and reveal his features. Two of the best in the 1906's were the Outlaw and the Zebra Kid. The kid didn't really need a mask as he was immediately identifiable by his 24 stone (152 kilos) bulk and his zebra stripped mask. The American outlaw wrestled in the U.K. most of the time. The crowd at Belle vue, Manchester had a great evening when the two hooded men were matched against each other. The contest went for 5 rounds before the large Zebra Kid landed awkwardly and twisted his ankle. The Outlaw seized his opportunity and wrenched a submission from his fellow countryman and was thus declared the winner. Zebra Kid, reluctantly peeled off his mask to reveal the face of the Greek-American George Bollas. The Outlaw continued to wrestle for a couple of years until injury forced him to retire from the ring keeping his identity a secret.

Another masked man who kept the crowd at fever pitch was Doctor Death. He featured in many a classic contest, using a combination of skill and unruly tactics to survive. He fought a number of other masked men who appeared on the scene disposing of then to quickly become the No.1 of his time. Doctor Death had a brutal bout against Doctor Blood at the West Ham Baths. It was Death who won and tore the mask off Dr Blood to reveal the face of Terry O' Neill. No sooner had this been done when another rival appeared to challenge him in the shape of the White Angel. They spent many months slagging each other off until the White Angel took the initiative by lodging £500 with the promoters (worth about £25000 today) and demanding a fight to the finish. The contest took place at Tooting Granada. Over 5000 fans watched a riveting bout, which swung first one way, then the other. After 15 hard fought rounds, 75 minutes of action, the White Angel, as much from exhaustion as from the heat of battle, collapsed and was counted out. Doctor Death was once again successful. The White Angel showed his face to be the south London star," Judo" Al Hayes. Hayes went on to become the Southern Area Heavyweight Champion for some years before moving to America, when he wrestled for a time as Lord Alfred Hayes. However, Al found he could make more money by commentating on T.V with his "posh" London accent which went down well in the States, rather than getting bruised inside the ring. Doctor Death continued wrestling for several years before going into promoting grappling himself. He had many successful promotions in which he fought for himself, before revealing his name as that of Paul Lincoln, the Welsh promoter.

It was mainly the Heavyweight division which had the Masked men, but there was one notable exception. That of the Red Scorpion. He wrestled in the North of England and Scotland taking on all comers in the lighter weights. He was 5 feet 3 inches tall, weighed 13 stone (82.5kilos) and had a 44 inch chest. The Scorpion was good to watch and always had the crowd on their feet, mainly rooting against him! He had a very successful run until he fell foul of the World Lightweight Champion, the legendary George Kidd.

The Scorpion had occasion to comment very unfavourably on the lightweight maestro in the national press, saying what he would do to the wee man from Dundee if he ever dared to face him. Never one to resist a challenge the side stake of £500 was placed by each grappler and the bout took place in Dundee. It was a real snorter. The crowd were not disappointed. The match ended when Kidd applied his much favoured "surfboard" hold, a move, which was banned on the continent, forcing the Scorpion to throw in the towel. When the mask was removed the crowd were astonished to see the face of Ted Heath from Leeds. He had been the partner to Alan Dennison in the formidable tag team of the Dennisons. Heath was an all action wrestler who had been involved in rugby league. His first team had been Bramley, later transferring to Keighley and subsequently ending up with Doncaster, before breaking into the world of wrestling.

But by far the greatest masked grapplers of all time were the legendary Count Bartelli and Kendo Nagasaki. Bartelli had been a masked star since he left the army in 1946. He had always been a keen physical culturalist who believed in weight training. His career behind the mask took off around 1950 and he remained undefeated and very successful for 16 years. Bartelli had met the best in the world travelling all round the globe as well as the length and breadth of the country. He was strong and fit. Unlike other masked men he was popular with the crowds and in his heyday, they flocked in their thousands to see him. His strong man stunts were talked about everywhere he went. He seemed invincible.

But in 1963 a new rival appeared on the scene. He went by the name of Kendo Nagasaki. He was 6feet 1 inch in height and his long black tights made him look even bigger. He weighed in at 16 stone (101 kilos). His ring garb was a traditional black samurai warrior's outfit complete with a red lined black cape, black and white striped mask and a ceremonial samurai sword. As the master of ceremonies was introducing him, Nagasaki would throw salt to the four corners of the ring, much like the Sumo wrestlers do in their very elaborate ceremony.

Once introduced, Nagasaki would race across the ring towards his opponents corner bringing down the razor sharp blade of the sword, stopping inches from his opponents face. If he ever had misjudged this his opponents head would have been split like a cabbage. The sword was real, and Kendo would often demonstrate its sharpness. This was real intimidation which often unsettled some of the hardest men. The final threat was the full eye length, deep red contact lenses which he wore giving his eyes a very sinister look. He was powerfully built and a master of Karate and Judo. Having only just begun his career in U.K. Nagasaki went campaigning in America and Japan. He learned many ideas and skills. It was not until he returned in 1965 that the promoter Arthur Wright thought this would make a brilliant contest. Nagasaki was beating all in his path recording some very notable wins. It was on the 6th March, 1966 at the Victoria Hall, Stoke on Trent the battle of the ring giants took place. This was the one the whole of the wrestling world had been waiting for, and it was indeed a cracker. Count Bartelli had always been popular, but in his local hall of the Victoria Hall he was considered a hero.

Bartelli trained extra hard for this contest and look very fit indeed. The Count had always had a reputation for his feats of strength but his well tuned body seemed even more indestructible. When he took to the ring the roar of support was deafening. No doubt he was the local hero. Then the electric atmosphere was charged with a dark foreboding when Kendo Nagasaki walked into the ring. He looked fearsome and sinister. The crowd shouted abuse and catcalls. This was the man they all wanted to see soundly beaten. As his manager George Gillette took the microphone to introduce his star, the sound of the crowd completely drowned him out. Nagasaki went through his usual samurai routine, racing across the ring and bringing the sword blade down centimetres from Bartelli face. To his credit, Bartelli didn't even flinch, however he must have felt inside. A psychological victory point to the Count.

Referee Stan Rylands then brought the two of them together, hurriedly relayed his instructions, then the contest was off. The battle went first Bartelli way then Nagasaki. It was close with both men giving of their best. The contest could have blistered the paintwork in that hall that evening, such was the excitement. After a series of weakening moves, the Count then applied his favourite hold, the arm wrench which had given him victory on so many occasions. As he hurtled Nagasaki across the ring he wrenched his arm and stopped Nagasaki dead in his tracks. The suddenness of the jolt dislocated Nagasaki's shoulder. It looked as if the contest was over. Kendo rose slowly from the canvass and the Count rushed in to finish the bout. However, as he did so, Kendo lifted him clean off his feet and threw Bartelli over the top rope sending him crashing down on top of the seats ten feet below. The fall was nasty and as Bartelli rose to his feet, his right knee which had troubled him so often throughout his career, gave way. Bartelli was in a great deal of pain. He failed to return to the ring and was counted out.

At the age of 43 years, Count Bartelli had finally been beaten. The referee Rylands untied the blood soaked mask, which had been saturated in sweat to reveal the face of Crewe businessman, Geoff Condliffe. The press surrounded the ring to capture the first pictures of the masked man who had had a successful run of 20 years without defeat. Bartelli's face was almost unrecognisable due to the severe bruising and cuts on his face.

Meanwhile, over in the other corner, the victor, Kendo Nagasaki was receiving a cheque for £1000. He had proved himself to be superior. So successful was Kendo, he went on to have an even longer run of success than Bartelli by remaining masked for 32 years. The only person who ever came close to beating him was the Bolton dynamo, Billy Howes who was the European Mid Heavyweight Champion at the time.

Howes was a grocer to trade but had considerable experience as a successful grappler. In 1967, during a televised contest, Howes gave Nagasaki a real pasting cutting the big man across his forehead. The blood pouring into his eyes prevented Nagasaki from seeing too well and Howes took full advantage. He tore off the mask to attack the head injury, but this was too much for Nagasaki who threw some powerful straight fingered chops to Howes throat and eventually brought Howes to his knees with a double-handed chop to the head. Kendo then swiftly left the ring before too many people could identify his facial features. His manager Gillette was later to claim Nagasaki removed the mask himself as he could not see, but I would dispute this.

Despite this set back, Kendo Nagasaki went on to beat the best in the world, even taking the North American Heavyweight title, and sweeping all before him.

Most unmasked wrestlers fade into obscurity. This was not the case with Geoff Condliffe, the Count. He recovered from his defeat and returned to his strict training routine. A year later at 44 years of age, he toured Australia and beat the Commonwealth Champion at heavyweight, Laurie Boyd, to become the oldest title holder the grappling game has seen. Whatsmore, he retained it, regularly putting it on the line for another 18 years before he retire through advancing years and several injuries in 1985. Count Bartelli had been wrestling for an unprecedented 47 years and had taken part in some 9138 contests. Believe me he was some fellah was Mr Condliffe, Count Bartelli.

These then were the greatest heavyweight masked men that the grappling scene has ever seen. Neither will ever be forgotten. My own spell as a masked man had been limited to hiding my face so that the independent promoters could use me. But I hated it. I found it very hot inside the hood and very restrictive in my line of vision.

Once I captured the Commonwealth Middleweight title I never even though about wearing a helmet again. The victory over Borg had given my confidence an enormous boost. I allowed all challengers to wrestle me for the championship. I ducked no one. In fact wrestling became a bit routine. The challengers came full of boasts unaware of my skills; and left beaten and bitterly disappointed. In the years between 1979 and 1981 I beat some of the biggest names in the business. Guys like Jon Cortez, Adrian Street, Mick McMichael, Jim Breaks, Jim McKenzie, Bobby Barnes, Zoltan Boschic and Jackie Pallo. Things seemed to be riding along on the crest of a wave as far as I was concerned. Until one night in Aberdeen when I faced a lad from Yorkshire who was to be my stumbling block. He was Mike Bennett.

Mike Bennett and I clashed in the ring one March evening at the Aberdeen Music Hall. I had never seen this as anything other than a normal contest. Bennett had been around the rings for several years longer than I had. He was as tough as teak, but then I had expected as much - after all, he was a Yorkshire man! We both climbed onto the ring: he looking very fit and agitated, I feeling a bit blaze. Given my track record and the wealth of experienced opponents I had seen off, Bennett seemed to be just another workman like grappler. It was not to be. The bout was fast and furious. I claimed the first fall in round 3, but Bennett equalized almost immediately in round 4. He then threw caution to the wind and hit me with everything but the kitchen sink! Before I could resist him, he gained a submission from a painful arm hold. Believe me I was only to glad to give in. Unfortunately, he spoiled his victory by smacking he square in the face with the water bucket when the M.C. was making the announcement. Bennett then threw in a few punches and Well-placed kicks to boot. Somehow I just felt drained. On the back of this Mike Bennett challenged me for my Commonwealth title. I was only to happy to give him the chance. I was determined to get back at him. My pride had been injured and I didn't like it one little bit!

Mike Bennett had always been a top line grappler. He had faced the best and beaten most. His fame first came in 1965 when as a teenager he entered independent Television's "World of Sport T.V. Trophy." His important televised win came when he defeated the much more experienced Spaniard Vento Castillo by breaking his jaw and forcing him to retire. This sensational win marked Bennett out from the rest of the crowd. It was Mike's father, who himself had been a boxer, that took young Mike along to see the grappling at the St Georges Hall in Bradford. He was only 14, but from that day on he was hooked. Mikes father being in the fight game himself, boxing under the name of "Digger Eric Bennett, knew referee Joe Hill and introduced him to Michael Joe in turn introduced Michael to weight training and in turn to amateur wrestling. Weighing only 9 stone (57 kilos) he went along to the Bankfoot Barbells Club to learn Judo. This was followed by amateur wrestling at the Hill Top Club. Amongst those who coached Michael was ring veteran Ernest Baldwin, himself a former Heavyweight Title holder. Baldwin noticed the keenness, enthusiasm and mental agility that marked him down as a young man going places. Today he stands 5 feet 9 inches tall and weighs 12 stone. (76 Kilos) Although he was trained as a welder, he much prefers the outdoor life and has spent much of his working life as a gamekeeper.

It is my firm belief that the only thing which stopped Mike Bennett being ranked as one of the greatest in the game was his wanderlust, to satisfy which, he took frequent breaks from his ring career. Nonetheless, he had wrestled and beaten the best around. Now he was coming for me.

It was in May 1981 that I entered the ring to face the redoubtable Mike Bennett with my title up for grabs. Bennett entered the ring first to a chorus of "Boos'." I followed with resounding echo of cheering. Clearly I was the favourite and the local hero.

Referee for the evening was Roy "bull" Davies. The first heavyweight wrestler I had ever seen on television. Much older now but very strict in the interpretation of the rules. Bennett refused to take off the ring on his fourth finger claiming it was stuck. Water and some pulling by Davies was employed but the ring refused to budge. I was given the opportunity to have the championship contest postponed until this problem could be resolved but I refused anxious as I was to get on with the bout. Eventually we were off. Both of us battled at a furious pace. When I gained a pin fall in round 4 Bennett went wild. He had already collected a public warning in round 3 for some dubious work on the ropes in round 5 he collected a second. I saw him pull away the corner post padding and made a determined attempt to avoid being posted into the corner. However, Bennett, as shrewd as ever picked me up and slammed me head first into the bare corner buckle. As I got to my feet feeling very groggy, he hit me with a barrage of blows from his hands and feet, which stunned me even further. Suddenly everything went red. Only then did I realise my head was cut open. Blood began to pour everywhere. The sweat making it worse. I could hardly focus on my opponent when I felt "Bull" Davies hand on my shoulder. He moved in to separate Bennett and me. My impression was that as Bennett had collected 2 public warnings and was a fall down, he referee would disqualify him for his rule bending. However, nothing could be further from the truth! Davies looked at my split head and stopped the contest awarding the title and belt to the aggressive Yorkshire man, Mike Bennett.

I was totally shocked. I protested bitterly to the referee, but his decision was made. Bennett could hardly believe his luck and began to parade around the ring holding the belt above his head to the sound of Abba singing," The Winner Takes it All." My sister Roslyn, who was sitting in the front row left the building in a state. More because of the cut than because I had lost the title. I was devastated. I left the ring, had a shower then drove off to the Aberdeen Royal Infirmary to have my injuries attended to. I was given 17 stitches in my forehead. It hurt like hell, but not as much as my pride. This was not the way to loose a title. I felt I had been the better wrestler and had been cheated by skulduggery.

Next morning I contacted the promoter and demanded a return contest. It had been agreed that there would be a 6-month return bout guaranteed if the Champion lost the title and I wanted to invoke that clause. Mr Brian Dixon agreed. However, the return contest did not go the way I had planned.

It was a hot summer evening in July 1981 when the Music Hall sold over 1200 tickets to fans desperate to see the return bout between Bennett and me. As the new Champion Mike Bennett was introduced first. He was in the blue corner with the British Flag behind him.

The crowd were very hostile towards him. But Bennett with his usual arrogant smirk was unmoved. The sound of Scotland the Brave hit the air and I ran into the ring confident and enthusiastic, with the partisan crowd fully behind me. then disaster struck.

As I climbed between the ropes I saw Mike Bennett rush towards me holding the Flag pole. The end of the pole had a brass pear shaped ornament, which was very sharp. As he charged towards me I stepped back and fell out of the ropes and onto the floor. I was livid. I tore off my ring jacket and rolled through the ropes on to my feet when I grabbed Bennett by the throat. What happened next could only be described as a street fight as we punched, chopped, kicked and butted each other. We rolled out of the ropes. Bennett grabbed the ringside bucket and smashed it over my head. In turn I grabbed him by the ears and bounced his head off the timekeepers table. As he got up I lifted him and slammed him down on that same table so hard that it broke in two. We fought our way back into the ring and as the referee and MC tried to stop us, I grabbed the microphone and twisted the cable round Bennett's neck. He was gasping for breath when the officials and two other wrestlers pulled me off a prostrate Mike Bennett. Needless to say the referee declared the bout null and void as both grapplers were considered to be out of control. But Bennett once again, achieved his ambitions and left the ring as Commonwealth Champion. It was a disgraceful 10 minutes of brawling and not one I would wish to repeat. Such were the passions aroused between us. Nothing had been resolved between us, but Bennett still retained the championship. How would I ever get the title back? Was this the end of my spell as an International Champion? Surely not.

Later on that month, I had two other contests following which, a surprise letter came to me. A promoter had billed me to appear in Meadow bank Stadium in Edinburgh. My opponent was to be none other than Mike Bennett. The promoter explained that this was not a title bout but it might help me re establish my claim as number one contender. I did not need to be asked twice. So in August of that year in Edinburgh I climbed into the ring to face yet again my arch rival. This had been big news all over Scotland and the fans turned out in force to see us battle it out. But surprisingly enough, and perhaps because we had so much respect for each others abilities, we wrestled for 6 rounds without breaking any rules. it had been a scientific contest, which the purists enjoy. Fast clever moves and counter moves, both of us trying to outsmart the other. Neither wishing to do anything, which might allow the other to score the advantage. Because neither of us managed to pin the other the contest was declared a drawn bout. the quality of grappling had been exceptionally high which showed the people that both of us could wrestle well and to a high standard. We both excelled ourselves that night. But he still remained champion and I still needed to settle the score.

The Kelvin Hall in Glasgow has seen some tremendous wrestling bouts. It was to experience yet another when Mike Bennett and I were contracted to wrestle each other. Bennett was determined to dispose of my challenges once and for all. He demanded a side stake of £500. Winner takes all. I agreed. However, he refused to put the title at stake claiming that I had had more than my fare share of attempts to wrest the title from him and as he had defended the title against me already it was not mandatory for him to put the belt on the line for another year. I accepted this simply because I wanted to get my hands on Bennett once again.

Again the contest was fast and furious. Rules were bent and caution thrown to the wind as we battled to get the better of each other. However, the contest ended when we both fell out of the ring and continued to fight with each other. The referee continued to count but we were obsessed with getting at each other and did not hear the referee count us both out. Again we had not settled the question of who would be the victor. At this point we both approached the promoter and asked for an all in no falls, no submissions, no referee, bout. The last man standing to be declared the winner. This was too good a promotion to be missed and the promoter booked us for just such a bout in September 1981 at the Aberdeen Music Hall. Neither Bennett nor I could hardly wait!

About this time I was taking a keen and active interest in local politics. I had joined the Labour Party in 1978, much to my fathers delight. He had done the same one returning home from the war in 1945. As an ex serviceman, he became the secretary of the Labour Party branch known then as the Holburn Ward. He had continued this until 1953 when he found working late into the evenings prevented him being so active in the local party and he had to give it up. My father was delighted to learn I had been adopted as the prospective candidate for the St. Nicholas Division. The elections were due in 1982 and I had been given a full year to win the seat off the conservatives. History will record that I did and it was the first Regional Council seat to switch from Conservative to Labour since the two tier system of Regional Councils were brought into being. Made even more remarkable by the fact that Margaret Thatcher was at her height and sweeping all before her at this time. However, that was to come.

In September 1981 I had an "ALL IN" bout against Mike Bennett. These type of contest were not seen very often in British Wrestling. Originally an American idea, they were used mainly to settle long-standing feuds between top grapplers. Andy Robbin had settled a feud with Abe Ginsberg through a "last-man-standing-wins" situation. They pleased the crowd and also the grapplers. The only rule is that no foreign objects are allowed. But there are no other rules, no pin falls or submissions. Only a knock-out can win the contest. The referee is only there to hold aloft the winners arm. In the crowd that evening was an old friend of mine called Freddie Burgess. He was seated right in the front row beside my corner. I hadn't seen him for ages, but what he did that night probably won me the bout.

Once again 1200 people packed into the Music Hall for this contest. Once again Bennett and I set about each other at a furious pace. In fact at one point I got so carried away I forgot it was an "ALL_IN" bout and actually pinned Bennett. The referee must have been similarly engrossed because he counted out the fall before realising it didn't count and ordered us to wrestle on. In the 26th minute the contest swung in my favour. Bennett floored me with a thumb to the eyes. He raced across the ring to my corner and tore off the corner pad. He then picked me off the floor and hurled me at the bare corner. It was at this point Freddie Burgess saw what was happening and lifted the he padding where he held it until I impacted against the ring corner. Bennett saw my cushioned posting and rushed in to quickly drag me off the canvas attempting to throw me once again into this corner. However, I managed to reverse the throw and hurtled Bennett into the corner post. Good old Freddie Burgess on seeing me switch the move, simply dropped the corner padding he was holding and Mike Bennett got the full force of the bare ring corner in his back. The very fate he had tried to set up for me.

Once he hit the corner I quickly followed him, picked him over my head and slammed him head first into the canvass. He suffered and injured shoulder and could not continue. I was declared the winner. It was such a relief. "Now," I told the promoter, grabbing the microphone from the M.C.,"I demand a return title shot." The crowd roared in approval and the promoter readily agreed.

I cannot remember much about that return title contest in November 1981, simply that defeat is bitter, but revenge is oh so sweet! The contest lasted for only 5 rounds and we were both very much up for it. The battle swayed first one way then the other. The pace was blistering. I gained a fall in round 3 which set Bennett off on a wholesale rule bending purge. But the end came in round 5 when I caught Bennett rushing me off the ropes. I lifted him into the air and body slammed him so awkwardly that he took the full force on his shoulder. He was in such distress he could not make the count of 10. Once again I was Champion of the Commonwealth.

This time I was to retain the title following 10 title defences until 1992 when I finally retired from the ring. I suppose the result was more than a little flattering from my point of view. The bout had been a lot closer than most people would have imagined.

Full marks to Mike Bennett. He was no slouch. In fact he went on the following year to beat World Champion at lightweight, Johnny Saint, form Blackpool to take that title for a year before loosing it back on a disqualification. Similarly Bennett defeated Brian Maxine for the British Middleweight Title and retained that also for around a year before he lost it again. Bennett's problem seemed to be his commitment to the game. He was always torn between his first love of Game keeping and his second Wrestling. frequently, and often after some superb victories in the roped square, the wanderlust would overtake him and he would pack his bags and return to full time Game keeping. Unfortunately this has prevented him from becoming one of the greats in the ring. Few grapplers can boast of victories over people like Alan Dennison, Jackie Pallo, Vento Castella, Brian Maxine and Johnny Saint. But Mike Bennett did exactly that. He had met and beaten some of the biggest names and always has done ever since his wrestling career began, by winning the golden gown award over Jon Cortez on ITV's World of Sport. Certainly his grappling abilities caused me no end of trouble and I will always remember his bouts. They had everything and brought out the best and worst in both of us. A few years later, the wanderlust again took over the life of Michael Bennett and he left these shores for New Zealand. Once there, he met and married a Maori girl named Prabah and they have a son called Shelvin. Last I heard he was back living and working on an estate in Wales. No doubt very happily settled at last.

My next title defence was against Peter Preston. He was a real bundle of energy much in the Marc Rocco or Billy Howes mould. Preston had risen to fame in the late 1960's when he appeared on television and became the first grappler to beat Mick McManus on television. Some thing, which rarely happened. Mind you it has to be said that many of McManus opponents were hand picked for television so they would be unlikely to give him much problems. But the story goes that some of the Northern promoters got a bit fed up with McManus gaining easy victories on television and wanted to put him under the same kind of pressure he often had to face in many of the halls round the country. So on this occasion the booked Peter Preston, who at that time was an unknown, although he had been wrestling for a number of years. McManus was conned into thinking that this was just another run of the mill opponent and accepted the contract to face Preston on television. the promoters had worked out with Preston that when the bout started, he should extend the hand of sportsmanship to McManus, and before he could decide to accept or reject it, Preston was to grab his legs and pin the unsuspecting McManus to give Preston the immediate advantage. A position Mick McManus hated, having to come from behind. Well it worked like a charm. McManus fell for it and was behind coming out for round 2. The bout continued at a fast and furious pace. By the end of round 4 it was clear to McManus that he could not win this 6 round contest unless he could knock out Preston. As Preston was too strong for this, McManus openly broke every rule in the book and got himself sent out in the 5th round. Some say this was the only way McManus could save face and he deliberately went out to be disqualified. Whatever the truth, McManus was beaten for the first time on Television by a disqualification, and Peter Preston became a household name. Preston continued to build a reputation often showing scant regard for the rules himself, (he claimed it was enthusiasm!) and using the surprise fall in the first round as a tactic found himself with victories over many of the top names in the sport.

In the early seventies, Preston further enhanced his reputation by teaming up with the veteran Welterweight Champion of Europe, Alan Colbeck from Wakefield, to form one of the most unlikely tag team pairings, yet one of the most successful of all time. known as the "Masters" Colbeck and Preston's styles combined to beat every top tag team including victories over well established teams like, "Hells Angels" the "Dennisons," The" Royal Brothers," and Mick McManus and Steve Logan. No mean achievement. I relished the challenge for my title from a guy like Peter Preston because he was a real scalp if you cold take it.

When we fought in the Kelvin Hall in Glasgow, Preston tried the surprise fall on me in round one, but as I had been well aware of this king of shock tactic I neatly grabbed his shoulders and turned him over for the count of three giving me the advantage straight away. The Scottish crowd went banzai. Preston went ape-shit. He used a spectacular leg submission move on me in round 3 to equalise the contest, but when he went for it again in round 5 I once again turned the tables on him and using his own leg submission move I gained the winning submission thereby retaining the title and belt. It was a furious contest but one I enjoyed winning. I considered the scalp of Peter Preston to be well worth collecting!

Following this I defended my title against Alan Dennison. Not the wild psycho he had once been but an older calmer Alan Dennison. He grappled well but lost the bout when I took 2 falls off him. The bout was not a spectacular one but the crowd loved it. I have always had a soft spot for Alan. Alan Dennison was a fitness fanatic. He was only 5'3" but because of his tremendous strength he was like a scaled down Hercules. He boasted a 47" chest with 16" biceps. As a physical culturalist he won many body building titles including Mr Yorkshire,

Mr Bradford and Mr North East Small Man! He trained with weights, jogging on the Yorkshire moors and throwing around large boulders. He used to train in a rented Gym, which he shared with his mate Geoff Portze.

When he started wrestling Dennison was a welterweight weighing in at just over 11 stone. At first he used his speed and skill to defeat opponents, but on realising his strength as an asset he switched to a much more aggressive style. This way he was able to compete on a par with the likes of Jackie Pallo, Mick McManus and les Kellet. Many grappling fans still remember his televised bout against Jackie TV Pallo. Following one liberty too many Dennison exploded and knocked out Pallo who had to be the carried from the ring still unconscious. Pallo remained that way for over 20 minutes. It was following this that he gained the nickname "Psycho" on account of his wild and uncontrollable temper. Unfortunately he was being disqualified as much as he was winning. In the 1960's Alan Dennison teamed up with Sid Cooper to form a very successful tag team partnership. However that success was surpassed when Cooper moved on and Dennison formed a new tag team partnership with Ted Heath. Both had similar interest and were keen body builders. Their battles with the likes of McManus & Logan, Colbeck and Preston, Adrian Street and Bobby Barnes, or the Royals were the stuff of legends. They will always be remembered by those fortunate enough to have seen them.

The team broke up when Heath moved to America. It was about this time that promoter Max Crabtree persuaded him to revert to his original style. Dennison lost something doing this but he did gain more popularity. His career was crowned in 1980 when he defeated Jim Breaks to take the British Welterweight Title of Great Britain. When I first met Alan Dennison he tried to persuade me to crop my hair, come into the ring in flip-flops and dye my skin yellow. He said I could pass myself off as a Japanese champion Not one of his brighter ideas. Needless to say I ignored him. It's funny how the fans made up their own ideas about wrestlers. I remember one telling me that Dennison had a metal plate in his head and when a wrestler touched his ears that moved the metal plate causing him sever pain. That's why he lost his head so often. Of course it's a load of bollocks but hey the man paid his money and could believe what he liked! I met Alan many times and I really enjoyed his company. He was no fool. Sadly Alan died following a TV bout aged only 52. He was a proper gent and a credit to the game. He had taken and interest and promoted many of the young stars of the ring and many were in his debt. The irony is that Alan had planned to retire 3 months after that fateful bout. Isn't life a bitch?

For the next few years I roamed around the rings of Scotland and the north of England putting my title at stake and allowing all comers to face me. It was great experience and to be fair, I rather enjoyed it. I kept my bouts down to two per month, much to the disgust of the promoters who wanted my services virtually every night! However, I wanted to maintain a level of fitness which would give me good performances each time I stepped into the ring. No-one would ever say that 'Ironside' gave them a poor showing. I maintained my speed and counter-holds to a high standard. To be honest, I also had a full time job to cope with and my commitment to the Grampian regional Council was becoming stronger as I gained more experience of the political scene.

People have often asked me what it was like to be knocked out. On the two occasions it happened to me they were both very different. But the one I hated most was between drew McDonald from Perth. He was an exciting new prospect from mid Scotland. Noticed at the highland Games by Max Crabtree. Max had been looking for someone from Scotland to place on his bills in the south of England. Because he had disenchanted so many Scots lads Max was forced to look for someone new. I suppose his idea had been to find a large fit Scotsman who would have filled the mould of the late Ian Campbell or Big Jock Cameron. These guys were heroes at home but considered villains of the worst kind with the English audiences. The highland games was not a bad place to look because Crabtree had after all discovered both Bill Ross and Andy Robbin there and they were incredibly impressive wrestlers and sportsmen.

Anyway, Drew (Andrew actually!)loved training for power lifting and was only too keen to be coached by the Crabtree. He worked hard and learned the skills well. Drew had a background of 'Games' grappling so he wasn't exactly a novice. For two years he was coached and skilled in the mat and his career was carefully guided by Max Crabtree. Unfortunately he was only being groomed to become a fall guy for 'Big Daddy' something he very much resented later on. However, when I saw him he was at the height of his rise to fame. Crabtree had decided to test the Music Hall in Aberdeen to see if the locals would still pay good money to see their bills. I went along out of curiosity. Well all the usual bouts took place and Big Daddy did his big splash to close the so called main event, but there was still one bout to come. The opponent for drew MacDonald had not arrived. Crabtree asked if there were any challengers willing to tackle MacDonald. Well, fool that I am, I could not resist. I was incredibly popular in Aberdeen and had always been used to taking on opponents who were heavier than me in catch weight contests. But this time I must have been carried away with myself.

The promoter agreed and I came out for the challenge. I was 11 stone 4lbs (71.6 kilos) and stood full height at 5 feet 3 inches. As I looked across the ring at the fuzzy black, Afro- haired man from Perth I had a realisation that Drew was just under 6 feet tall and weighted 25 stone. (158 Kilos) Not to be outdone I had a game plan, which I thought would tire the Giant out. And, true to form I did so for 4 rounds. I nipped between his legs, I climbed over his back, tripped him up using all my speed and skill till came a silly mistake. In round 5 MacDonald caught me threw me into the ropes and as I rebounded I launched myself into a flying cross press.

On an opponent of my own weight this would have winded him and forced him to the canvas. However, on Mad MacDonald it was simply a convenient way to catch me hoist me high into the air and administer a power slam backed by 25 stone of flesh, muscle and bones. It was as if the lights went out suddenly and a strong crushing pain crossed my chest. ten minutes later in the dressing room big Drew himself was leaning over me congratulating me on a great contest. I did my utmost but there was no way I could give away that sort of weight advantage and win. Nonetheless I had a go and kept the big lad at arms length for over 22 minutes. Pity he caught me in the end!

Following this clash with a titan, I returned to wrestling men my own size. After all, isn't that why weight divisions had been introduced in the first place? I was content to take on the best around until I was booked to grapple at the Kelvin Hall in Glasgow against the then World Lightweight Champion Johnny Saint. He had originally been billed to face Jim Breaks but an injury robbed the Glasgow crowd of that contest this time. However, It gave me a chance, quite unexpectedly to face the main man of the Lightweight division. I did so and stopped him with a wrist injury in round 3. Suddenly the gateway to the World Championship seemed as if it were about to open! Wasting no time I threw down the gauntlet. But Johnny Saint was none too keen. He said he would put the title on the line only if I could prove this win was not a fluke! Eight weeks later we met again in the Kelvin Hall, Glasgow. Again an enthralling bout where I needed all my skill and guile but despite Saint gaining the opening fall, I countered one of his favourite moves to take an equalising fall in round 3 then forced his retirement in round 4 when he submitted to my own version of a leg lock called a twists and stretch. Encouraged by the partisan crowd in Glasgow I now demanded the title shot. His time Saint could do little but accept. A couple of months later, in my hometown of Aberdeen City Council I faced Johnny Saint at the Beach Ballroom. Why I didn't go for the Glasgow venue I cannot quite remember. It seemed logical that if I were to win the world title I should do it in my hometown. I also had an election coming up for the local council where I was standing as a Local Councillor And people advised me this would be a tremendous Publicity boost. So on April 1986 I *set out to make history.*

Johnny Saint has always been a great grappler. Dedicated to fitness and his craft he was a true professional. But since winning the title following the retirement of George Kidd, he had been persuaded to try to emulate the great maestro. I believe this spoiled his own record and appeal but he followed, wrongly in my opinion, the advice of promoter max Crabtree. Now against other wrestlers copying the George Kidd moves was very successful, but having been trained by the great man himself, I had forgotten more of Kidd's moves than Johnny saint ever knew. Hence the reason he failed to beat me on 3 occasions. I could counter his counters before he was aware of it! Those people who saw our famous bout in Aberdeen will never forget it. Some say it was a classic. Others, the best they ever seen. The contest took place in the Beach Ballroom in Aberdeen. The normal venue, the Music Hall was closed for refurbishment. The place was full as over 1200 people enjoyed the evening's bouts. I entered the ring first as the challenger. Huge roars from the crowd. The enter Saint the Champion, a few boos and cat calls, all quite unnecessary, but a sizable cheer from the many battle worthy public. The referee gave our instructions; we shook hands then came out fighting. I was disappointed with My performance that evening. I believe I started too slowly. I was cagey and desperate not to loose any silly falls. Saint felt the same. But unlike his usual bouts he was unable to control me or to dictate the pace of the contest. We battled hold for hold, counter for counter and truly it was a contest for the connoisseur. Then in round 10 Saint found a lucky fault in one of my manoeuvres and quick as a cat seize the opportunity and pined me for the first fall. I was so disappointed. I could feel my chances slipping away. When the bell rang for the 11th round I tore across the ring and fought like a tiger tearing an equalizing submission from Saint after only 2 minutes. The home crowd were elated at this levelling of the bout.

Many thought I should have fought like that from the first round. But I was too cautious. When final bell for the final round 12 rang; I felt I had nothing to lose. I battled hard overwhelming Saint with body slams, postings and dropkicks. I punished his back and he was clearly weakening. Following up quickly I turned Saint over onto his stomach and heaved at his legs to deliver a full Boston crab. I felt every sinew of my body strain to force on that Boston Crab. I felt the referee tap me several times on the shoulder. I had not heard the bell ringing. For a moment I thought I had won, but the ref said Saint did not submit and the time had run out. I was bitterly disappointed yet thoroughly satisfied at my efforts. I shook Saints hand and asked for a return bout. Saint said perhaps, in the rings of England near his home. But we never met in the ring again. Despite the drawn contest it was one of my most satisfying bouts and one I shall never forget.

The next 2 years I spent wrestling for various promoters including my old pal Andy Robbins who was showing off his Bear Hercules. Many grapplers laughed at Andy when He said he would tour the country wrestling a bear. But Andy had the last laugh. He made a fortune. Enough to build his own Castle in Dollar.

In 1986 I had a strange opportunity. I was to wrestle for the European Lightweight Title. At that time it was held by Cry-baby Jim Breaks. Ten years earlier we had met on a Televised bout. I had between Breaks on a couple of occasions since and promoter Peter Keenan wanted me on his spectacular Kelvin Hall Bill. Unknown to me, Two weeks before the bout, Breaks had been beaten for the title by Jackie Robinson from Manchester. A cousin of the great Billy Robinson. Jackie was fast and fit. He could be relied on for giving the crowd value for money. In many ways he reminded me of Bobby Ryan who was a similar style and whom I had beaten in some of the Scottish Halls. When I was told it was Robinson I had to face I was rather worried. Although he was not the rule bender Breaks had become, he was nonetheless a clever wrestler and not likely to be easily manovered into loosing the place. The bout was a great one. Jackie as I suspected came out fast and furious. But a missed dropkick in the third round gave him problems from which he never recovered. I forced him to submit in round 4 and again in round 5. The result was not a true reflection of the contest as when we met subsequently the contest were very much closer although Robinson had never been able to beat me. So it was I lifted the European Lightweight wrestling title at Glasgow Kelvin Hall. The crowd who were always very partisan carried me round the arena on their shoulders. They fair loved it when their man won! I agreed to give a return bout within the year. I couldn't arrange anything sooner as I had to put up my Commonwealth Title against King Ben. That was in November 1986 and I thought it was a good warm up for the defence of the European crown albeit at a different weight. Having beaten King Ben rather convincingly I expected Robinson to be slightly easier. However fate as ever intervened. The Return bout against Robinson had been set for Aberdeen Beach Ballroom in May 1987.

In March of that year my involvement in local politics meant I had to head a trade mission on to Houston, USA promoting the businesses in the North East of Scotland at the worlds largest Oil Show. I contacted the promoter and told them. They were angry and said they could not cancel the bout as it was one of there main contests. I regrettably had to pull out of the match. The saddest thing from that was that the board of control which is mainly made up of wrestling promoters anyway, stripped me of the European Lightweight title and brought in Jim Breaks to face Jackie Robinson for the vacant title. It was the worst way to loose a title. I believe that titles can only be won and lost in the ring- never in a boardroom! That incident really burned me up and I will never forgive the antics of promoters that evening! The result was that Breaks won back the European title from Jackie Robinson and I was left with the Commonwealth middleweight title only. I defended my Commonwealth Title on 5 occasions beating Terry Jowett, a real wrestlers wrestler and greatly underrated, Bobby Barnes the other half of the Hells Angels Tag team, Mike Flash Jordon who was also a very clever grappler, Mal Sanders a former European Middleweight champion and Peter Preston, the barnstorming middleweight who always gives good value for money. I enjoyed a great tag team contest in Aberdeen where I partnered Frank "Chic" Cullen against the Mean Machine Roller ball Marc Rocco and Irishman Rocky Moran. It was memorable for many reasons. Firstly we won the match, though it has to be said Rocco took a fall off me, I equalized against Moran, and then Cullen took the winner off Moran. Secondly, I had always wondered what it would be like facing Rocco in the ring and that was my only chance. I would hardly describe it as a pleasant experience! And thirdly because it was partnering the lad I had helped into the professional ranks, Frank Cullen. He had grown considerably in stature and was a very clever grappler. In fact the British Heavy middleweight Champion. I was so pleased with his progress. He has certainly lived up to his early prospects. I have a lot of respect for the man.

New challengers like Robbie Brookside, Danny Collins, and Ian "Doc" Green were emerging, as was young Kid McCoy the son of King Ben. The world of grappling was changing and new blood coming in. I always welcomed the chance to face rising stars.

But one of my most interesting bouts happened at a place called Huntly where I wrestled for a George MacDonald from Elgin. I had been on second and finished my bout when George told me two wrestlers due to face each other in the final contest had not appeared. Could I help him out? I agreed so just before interval I came out and threw down a challenge to anyone in the crowd who would like to face me over 6 rounds. For a moment it seemed there were no takers, Then from out of the back of that dark smoky hall a young farmer appeared. He was 6feet 2 inches tall and built like a brick farmhouse! He said he weight in at 18 stones. The prospect of facing me at 5 foot 3 inches tall in my stocking soles and weighing a mere 11 stone 12 lbs must have been tempting. Obviously I had to accept the challenge and the young farmer was taken to the dressing rooms to find some wrestling gear that would fit him. Three contest later that night, and I found myself stretching up to see the whites of his eyes! The bell rang and I took off. I knew that if this guy got hold of me he would squeeze the life out of me. So I ran round him, through his legs, over his back, tripping him up and working on his legs. I drop kicked him, used the ropes impetuous to land a couple of elbows on his head. I threw chops, back elbows and flying head butts. I extended him for two rounds then I moved in and grabbed a leg twist submission, which I held onto for longer than I should have, forcing him to retire when the bell rang for round 3 he couldn't come out. Boy was I relived! But full marks to him. I was a professional fighter and he was simply a strong man. He at least had the guts to have a go.

1988 was a sad year for British grappling. Since the mid eighties various promoters were given a chance to put their stars on television. But the standard was extremely poor. The quality of the halcyon days of the 60's and 70's had gone. Many who appeared on TV were simply blimps, with little skills let alone a personality, put in the ring as cannon fodder for Big Daddy and Haystacks who by this time were well past their best. I always felt that TV should be the showcases of the game not the Christmas pantomime come early. We should have screened "big" fights, title contest, showcasing the best in British grappling. Not the show for the kiddies, which it rapidly became. There were fewer and fewer appearances of real grapplers like Danny Collins, Steve Grey, Fit Findlay, Marc Rocco, Marty Jones, Pete Roberts and Tony St Clair. Genuine guys who always gave 100% in the ring. Real masters of their craft. Many of them went abroad to wrestle where the money was better. There were no good heavies anymore. Most had retired. Pat Roach who was never a crowd puller and little heard of when gutsy heavies like Rocky Wall, Mal Kirk, Gwyn Davies, Billy Robinson, Steve Veidor, and Kendo Nagasaki were in their prime, was now considered a star. Don't get me wrong. Roachie was a very nice fella. He was always polite and willing to do anything for new grapplers learning their craft. But he never had any star quality, and was boring to watch which is why the crowd often booed him despite his reluctance to break any rules. Pat Roach lived on the reputation of appearances in Aufweidersen Pet. However, to be fair he did start up a wrestling gym for youngsters interested in taking up the sport. It was a sad day when the big "C" caught up with him. No matter how big you are if you get a bad dose of cancer it takes over. Poor Roachie.

Having seen the quality of wrestling quickly degenerating into a farce, and falling viewing figures Especially amongst young people, the new head of programmes for ITV pulled the sport off the screens. The grappling game, which had first appeared in 1955 in black and white monochrome television sets and captured the imagination of the public, now in 1988 was to be screened no more. The wrestling saga which for 33 years had brought the country to a standstill around 4 o' clock sadly now Bit the dust. The effect of this was to impact upon the audiences round the country. Some household manes like Marc Rocco, Marty Jones, and Tony St Clair pulled in the crowds. But when you are not in the TV public's eye they soon forget.

As the nineties began many promoters had thought they should try to emulate the American Grappling Scene. Although it was a total farce and admitted to being so, they ran it like a soap opera. People were left hanging on a hook desperate to tune in next week to find out what was going to happen to a certain grappler, or a tricky no-way-out situation. It had what real grappling in Britain never had. It had hard marketing, loads of promotional material, and plenty of dollars spent looking after the "stars." There are some real American wrestlers who can wrestle but they are few and far between. The actual wresting is reduced to a few minutes and the build up goes on for weeks. Everything is reduced to the lowest common denominator. I am afraid I don't like it. But as a TV spectacle you have to hand it to the Americans. Some of our young stars gave up the gruelling circuits of the UK to opt for the showbiz life offered in America. A far cry from the 60's and 70's when British Wrestlers were feared by the Americans and they literally went into hiding, One of our greatest heavyweights, Billy Robinson had to stay there for nearly 8 years before the top stars would face him in the ring. Such was his fearsome reputation.

I only wrestled three times in 1990 and once in 1991. In that bout I faced the young star Kid McCoy. He was fast and fit. It was a really good contest for the purists. However it ended in a 6 round draw. I found it tough. Later on I analysed the contest in my mind and I realised that I could make excuses about not being fully Fit, or that McCoy whom I beat twice in 1989 had vastly improved, which was true. But the bottom line for me was that I felt I would be really hard pushed to beat him even on a good day. My time in the grappling game had come and gone. My era was at an end. I resigned my Commonwealth Title and retired from the ring. I did lace up my boots for another bout in 1992 but for me it was more like an exhibition bout pitting myself against a newcomer whom I beat on experience. I have never wrestled since.

My 20-year career in wrestling which began in the 1970's was now at an end. I was fortunate to join grappling scene at a time when some of the biggest stars of the 1960's were just past their peak and beginning to wane. I had beaten many great grapplers like Dave Fit Findlay, Tommy Billington, and Davey Boy Smith on their way up the ladder of success at a time when they were very much lighter. Now has been the young challenger, who jumped the ring to throw down the gauntlet, I had to recognise that newer younger guys were coming along and they had ambitions too. My era and the great years in wrestling had come and gone.

Throughout my grappling career, two questions have always been asked of me. Who was the best grappler and is it all fixed. Well I can only comment on my time in classic UK wrestling. There are several contenders. Billy Robinson from Manchester was a strong technical wrestler. Mike Marino, so long the World Mid Heavyweight champion, was considered a wrestlers wrestler. He lived the game and knew every hold in the book. Andy Robbins the Commonwealth Mid Heavyweight Champion from Auchterarder. Not so clever technically but a powerful wrestler who moved as fast as a lightweight, and overpowered his opponents. Very Charismatic, larger than life guy. Kendo Nagasaki a fierce grappler with enormous amount of moves who terrified his heavyweight opponents. Marty Jones, a great amateur who moved into the professional ranks with ease and quickly became a champion. And Tommy Billington known as the Dynamite Kid. The greatest grapplers of his generation and with both speed and scientific skills moved Wrestling into a new phase with many wrestlers throughout the world inspired by him and desperate to copy him. Internationally known and quite brilliant. The man in my view who shaped wrestling in the 1980's, 1990's and into the millennium with people like Chris Beniot modelling his style on him.

To answer the first question, the greatest of all time, I need only look 60 miles south of my home in Aberdeen. To the man of a 1000 holds from Dundee, the Houdini of the ring, the man who was World Lightweight Champion for 26 years, George Kidd. George was a wrestler wrestler. He had a fit body and an equally fit mind. He could out think as well as out wrestle opponents who were anything up to 5 stone (31.7 kilos) heavier than himself. At his peak he stood 5foot 4 inches tall weighting in at 10stone 10 pounds (68 kilos) He perfected a style, which used the strength of his opponents against themselves. It was a special technique based on the Greco-roman style of wrestling. When I trained with him in the early 1970's he was I his 50's. I was superbly fit yet I couldn't beat him.

He was born in Dundee in 21/2/25. He was an apprentice joiner to trade in his hometown. He left Dundee to join the Royal Navy as a mechanic during the Second World War. He began grappling seriously in the late forties on leaving the Fleet Air Arm. He claimed the Scottish Lightweight title in 1947, the British Title in 1948 and the European title in 1949 and finally the world lightweight championship in 1950. A title he won beating the Mexican Rudi Quarrez. The Lightweight Championship of the World, which after 26 years and over 1000 contest, 49 title defences He retained successfully until he retired in 1976. Unprecedented in any sport. He met all the best "stars" of the ring defeating people like Legendary Mick McManus, Jackie Pallo, Alan Colbeck, Adrian Street, Jon Cortez, Eddie Cappeli, Ken Joyce and Zoltan Boschic. George wrestled at lightweight. He trained with weights, and running.

His greatest asset, the thing that kept him supple enough to slipping and out of holds was his dedication to Hatha yoga. Good for mind concentration and great for keeping the body in condition. It was a fact that many people used to claim that "he must be double jointed!" because of the easy with which he used to escape from intricate and painful locks and holds clamped on by experienced strong men who were experts in their field. George loved a challenge and even in his twilight years he insisted in tackling the up and coming youngsters of the day, many of whom tried to copy his style. Characteristically George used to say that imitation is the best form of flattery. Though some of the grapplers used to claim that at one point George got so fed up with imitators trying to copy his special moves, that he Insisted that the promoters keep the other wrestlers locked inside their dressing rooms until his contest was over. However I find this hard to believe. When the legendary world middleweight boxing champion, Sugar Ray Robinson came to Dundee, Scotland, it was the maestro George Kidd who was chosen to show him round and to get involved in some pretty rigorous training sessions with the man. George was dedicated to success in the ring and he gave 100%. He was a study of concentration giving up flashy gimmicks, which he claimed made the game into a circus or pantomime, and colourful ring gear for a plain black pair of trucks and boots. He let his extraordinary style of pure scientific ring craft do the talking for him. He was a joy to watch. The quality of his wrestling spoke volumes, applying many holds, which he created himself, and never using the same move twice in any contest.

Outside the ring George was a down to earth individual full of fun, stories and impersonations of his favourite film actors. He was a snappy dresser. He often wore an overcoat, suit and brief case. He was world champion and dressed accordingly. Many would say it was his wife Hester to whom he was dedicated who kept him on the right track. I have no doubt that was true as he went to great lengths to care for her. On one occasion he chased a bus through the streets of Dundee to catch up with a driver who insulted Hester at a bus stop. Needless to say George put him right! Kidd was so popular that at one time he was given his own weekly TV show on Grampian Television called "The Wednesday People" which was so successful that it was followed by another show simply titled "THE George Kidd Show" and a quiz series which he hosted. Always up for a challenge the late Ron Thompson, a broadcaster with Grampian television used to tell folk about the time in the studio when George Kidd would challenge anyone to try to keep him in a hold from which he could not escape. One time a cameraman, who had been in the marines, weighing 16 stone and was determined to take up the challenge. He held George for several minutes but Kidd managed to escape. It was a tougher battle than usual, as when he arrived home his wife Hester was concerned about his white shirt being covered in blood!

For a spell in 1973 –1976 I often travelled with him to venues in Perth, Glasgow and Edinburgh. He loved to recount tales of his earlier days in the grappling game. They could fill a book on their own. Kidd was also known for his generosity to charities. Grapplers themselves used to tell tales like the time when Former World Middleweight Boxing Champion Randolph Turpin tragically committed suicide. Kidd sent on £500 to help the family through their hard times. Though a household name in grappling long before it became popular through the medium of television, George seldom appeared on the Saturday afternoon programme World of Sport. He believed that this detracted from the spectator who paid their money and came along to the local halls. He also felt that TV never gave the proper rate for the job. Given that Over 11 million television viewers tuned into the wrestling every Saturday, when it was at its height, George felt a mere £60 was not nearly a proper percentage of the gate! His special moves were to roll up in a ball like a hedgehog leaving his opponents confused as to how they could unravel him and the surfboard. The surfboard was eventually banned in Europe because when Kidd applied it there was no alternative but to submit. Few men carried on after its application.

George was one of life's great characters. Dedicated to his ring craft, his wife Hester, and their son (whom I never met) It was following Hester's death that George finally retired from the ring in 1976. In his last week of wrestling he beat, Adrian Street, Marc Rocco and Steve Logan. His record has never been equalled let alone beaten. Nor has his style ever been successfully copied though many have tried. He was one of Scotland's greats and I was proud to know him. Unfortunately we may never see his like again.

Now the Million-dollar question- is it fixed. I have heard this one so many times. There are two camp of thought. One says it's all faked; the other says it's all genuine- the truth lies somewhere in the middle. To say that the contest is rehearsed is ridiculous. Wrestlers travel all over the country to different venues every week facing a range of opponents. It would be impossible to practise with each other as has often been suggested. In fact I believe much of my success was due to the fact that because the other wrestler from the south hadn't heard of me, they assumed I would be a push over. Little did they know? Some claim the showmanship is the fake. Well showmanship is in every sport, be it tennis, boxing, football or wrestling. Some do it to draw attention to themselves and keep themselves in the eye of the sporting public. People always remember a character better than a nonentity. The general rule was if you won you got a full wage packet is you were disqualified you got expenses only. Promoters only wanted to book winners. Why would anyone want to "throw" a bout. The only time I saw something close to that was when a former star had aged and was not doing as well as he used to. He had been out drinking and wasn't really fit to enter a rind. When the bell rang he ran out, his opponent grabbed his wrist and our bold hero simply fell onto his back where he laid until the referee counted him out. Sad but true. That's the closest I have ever come to that. Sure some wrestlers lay it on thick when they are under attack from their opponent- it the best way of getting them to come in close and turn the tables. When Mick McManus had an injured knee he would put the bandage on the opposite knee to throw opponents off the scent. Good tactics. There have been occasions when wrestlers have been "carried" through a bout. This usually happens when the opponent is of a much poorer standard than yourself. Rather than disappoint the crowed the experienced grappler would lower his game to make the match last, longer and to give himself a workout. But that's not fixing a bout. I recall a conversation with Jumping Jim Moser who went on TV in a catch weight contest. He was in with someone who was never a real match fir him but he ended the contest in 2 rounds. Given that TV is great exposure I was surprised and ask how this happened. Jim said well I had diarrhoea and as I came out for the second round I dropped my guts. Unfortunately I could feel the wetness seeping through my trunks, which were white in colour! Now do you understand! Good on yer Moser!!

Anyone who has seen the brilliance of the Dynamite Kid (Tommy Belington) and see him now in a wheelchair through his injuries it would be utterly mindless to try and tell him it was all fixed. Tommy did it all. He was a great stylist, tackled the Japanese, conquered Europe and went into the rings of America. I feel very sorry for the way things worked out for him. He gave so much enjoyment to people all over the world and has disadvantaged himself. God bless you Tommy.

I would swear in any court in the land that I have never taken part in a fixed fight. Others can speak for themselves. If you really want to find this out get in the ring and try it for yourself. I am disappointed however the way that wrestling degenerated in the 1980's ultimately leading to the TV bosses talking it off the air. Some unscrupulous promoters would bill things like Nick Mac Manus- a chip off the old block- unfortunately for the public nothing to do with the legendary Mick McManus. Or King Kendo – not the fearsome original Kendo Nagasaki but a very poor imitation. I think that the fact some promoters actually encouraged this was quite shameful. There occasions when the ring was put up with two young guys who had an interest in wrestling. Unscrupulous promoters would ask them to wrestle each other ion the last contest to let the "stars" get showered and off home. Naturally the crowd got a very substandard contest and left the halls feeling disappointed. Some promoters like Orig Williams, who used to wrestle as El Bandito, tried innovative things. When he secured the TV rights for the welsh version of Channel 4 Orig tried to introduce amateur wrestling and various styles of grappling used throughout the UK, but it was too little too late. At least he tried. Others used the women wrestlers as a gimmick to draw in the crowds, but that only lasted for a short time. The cleverer more genuine grapplers went abroad to wrestle in Japan or Europe where there was still a large following. Some promoters tried to introduce "American style" wrestling but again it was a pale shadow of the bombastic soap opera stars of the USA. It doesn't go down well. The USA admits theirs is a show. It cannot be a show and genuine grappling at the same time. And tragically, here in Britain they still haven't learned the art of marketing and public relations. The reason why the USA grappling works is because people know its all pantomime. The story lines are built up over 10 –12 weeks culminating in a showdown heading the top of a spectacular bill. It's not just a ladder match here, and a cage match there, with a royal rumble thrown in for good measure. When the American style under Vince McMahon came to Britain, Jackie Pallo said, "give it 10 years and it will be over. The pubic will be wanting something different." Well it's been nearly 30 now and there no sign of any dipping of fortunes. Mainly because they encourage new followers. I think the public would have still enjoyed original British style classic grappling, had we produced more action packed guys like Rocco, Tommy (Dynamite Kid) Billington, Marty Jones and Dave Findlay. There are a whole host of new younger stars who with coaching and encouragement, from ex grapplers, like John Naylor, Keith Hayward etc would be able to revive the Grappling

Game in the UK. The American way will run its course and people will be looking for something better. Mark my words.

To this day I have never regretted my life in the grappling game. It kept me fit and took me to all sorts of places I might never have been, and gave me experiences I might never have had. All sorts of people have been attracted to the squared circle to grapple. There have been Ministers of Religion, Policemen, Teachers, Civil Servants, Ballet Dancers, Chefs, and accountants and so the list goes on. Some folk ask is it fixed. Well my answer is have a go yourself and see. I have changed many minds by accepting their challenge to face me in the ring. Sure there is showmanship, it's the lifeblood of any sport and that keeps the fans interest. Of course there is playing to the crowd-that works the crowd up, gets them going. But at the end of the day they got in that ring to face an opponent and to win the match. The promoters don't pay losers.

I have often been asked who my personal favourite is. Well there are so many. For sheer excitement guys like Andy Robbins, Bill Ross, Marc Rocco, Mary Jones. For Skill Steve Wright, Tommy Billington the dynamite kid, Clayton Thomson, Alan Miquet, Jon Cortez, Monty Swann, Ken Joyce, Terry Jowett, Frank Chic Cullen. The best heavyweights must be Billy Robinson from Manchester and Peter Thornly-Kendo Nagasaki. Both were skilful, both were feared by other wrestles, and both had a never-say-die attitude. Andy Robbins didn't have the vast wrestling repertoire like them but he was fast and incredibly strong. People like Alan Colbeck, Jackie Pallo, and Mick McManus made the lighter weights respectable. Their contribution to the game can never be underestimated. But the greatest of all time, pound for pound has to be George Kidd. He was clever, could outsmart his opponents mentally, created over 1000 holds of his own, and was delightful to watch. Men like Les Kellet and Kevin Connelly were funny to watch because they had such great timing. But George did it all by skill. Even today people are emulating the moves or variations on a theme of the skill he alone brought into the grappling game. Aye, When will we see his like again? I enjoyed with most fans the speciality holds and counters of the grapplers. Julian Maurice and his spinning back breaker; Jim Breaks Arm Lift submissions; Albert Rocky Wall's flying head but: Tibor Szaczsh back hand chop: Mike Marino's small package pin fall: McManus and Logan's forearm smashes; Les

Kellet's swinging headlock: Marc Rocco's Pile driver: Andy Robbins Powerlock; and George Kidd's surfboard. Special moves which they perfected and which became their trademark. All guaranteed to finish any contest.

    I have made many friends and a few enemies in the ring over the years. But I would do it all again. I'd like to thank all the promoters who had faith in me and gave me a chance to show off my skills on their bills. George Relwyskow, Max Crabtree, Brian G. Dixon, and ex boxing champion Peter Keenan. I'd like to thank all the wrestles who faced me in the ring- it takes two to tango! I'd thank all the guys who gave me advice, gave me friendship and made my world a happier place. Grapplers like Alan Dennison, Monty Swann, George Kidd, Andy Robbins and Bill Ross. And finally you the wrestling public. Without you the whole journey would have been pointless.